Endorsements for
NIGHT WATCH

You have in your hands a book that, if used regularly, will change
your life. The Word says "His sheep hear His voice." God is speaking
to His church today. It's time we hear and discern what the Spirit is
saying to us. This book will teach you how to hear what the Lord is
saying to you while you sleep. Russ Moyer explains in detail how to
hear His voice. God often speaks to us in symbols. In the glossary,
these symbolic images are clearly explained. This book is a must for
every believer who receives or wants to receive revelation from the
Lord. I highly recommend this book along with a notebook and pen
by your bedside.

REV. JOHN IRVING
Pastor, The Gathering Place

There has been a need for a long time in the Body of Christ for
information concerning dreams and interpretation of our dreams.
While we know there can be abuse in this area, we know God has
always, throughout time, spoken to man through dreams. Throughout the Old and New Testaments we find dreams are a great part of
the Bible. God gifted Daniel and others in interpreting dreams. I
believe Russ Moyer is a man gifted and anointed in this hour for the
ministry of dreams and interpretation. This book Russ has written
contains valuable insights and knowledge of how to receive what the
Lord wants you to receive from dreams and interpretations. Russ is a
man of God who has great integrity and experience and puts into
practice what he has written in this book. I know it will be very
valuable to you in your walk with God.

REV. PAUL WETZEL
Pastor, Courts of Praise Fellowship

Russ Moyer, my dear friend, has once again blessed me personally with the writing of this book. He has an incredible ability to touch the heart, mind, and understanding of each person he meets. God has given Russ an ability to create a hunger to be free through deliverance and direction for our lives through dream interpretation as well as the wonderful way he has of exposing the gifts God has given us in the prophetic. Everyone has a past and a future. How to get it clean and keep it clean takes understanding of the Word. This book will be a guide to achieving great success in our lives. Thanks, Russ, for caring enough, taking the time with love, to help us make things happen that will change our lives and challenge us to grow as persons to reach our maximum potential.

JOAN GIESON
Ministries of Love and Healing Rooms of St. Louis

Brother Russ's book on dreams is an excellent book that is very teachable. It brings you into a greater understanding that God speaks through dreams and visions and it teaches you how to seek God for the interpretation. I highly recommend it.

REV. JANE LOWDER
Calvary Campground, Ashland, Virginia

NIGHT WATCH

*Unlocking Your Destiny through
Dreams and Visions*

RUSS MOYER

FOREWORD BY JOHN KILPATRICK

Published by:
McDougal Publishing
P.O. Box 3595
Hagerstown, MD 21742-3595
www.mcdougalpublishing.com

ISBN 1-58158-096-7

Printed in the United States of America
For Worldwide Distribution

Eagle Worldwide Enterprises
P.O. Box 39
Copetown, ON, L0R 1J0
Canada

Tel.: (905) 308-9991
Fax.: (905) 308-7798
E-mail: enterprises@eagleworldwide.com
www.eagleworldwide.com

Cover design by Mave Moyer, inspired by the Holy Spirit in a dream with the title and picture of the northern lights in Canada

DEDICATION

I want to dedicate this book to my wonderful wife, Mave, who put up with my nighttime antics, light and sound shows, talking in my sleep, and wrestlings with the Holy Ghost. Most importantly, for being my loyal and faithful friend, ministry partner, and helpmate. She believed and saw God in me when most others didn't. She is talented and gifted and has a ministry in her own right, but with unselfish love has always been willing to lay down her own desires and dreams to grab hold of the vision that God has put in me.

ACKNOWLEDGEMENTS

First, I would like to acknowledge my pastor, Paul Wetzel, of Courts of Praise Fellowship, Pensacola, Florida. He has always encouraged me to share my dreams and visions, and he first gave me a platform to move in the prophetic gifting that God had placed in my life while I served as an elder in his church.

Secondly, I would like to acknowledge the late Ruth Ward Heflin, who was a prophetess to the nations. It was an honour and a privilege to work with her. She encouraged me and gave me the freedom to operate in my gifting, under a powerful corporate anointing, in a spiritual environment where there was liberty as well as reverence for the spoken Word of God.

Thirdly, I would like to acknowledge Ira Milligan, a prophetic pioneer in his time, whose work I used to set a foundation and develop a vocabulary with the Lord. His book, *Understanding the Dreams You Dream*, was a tremendous piece of training material, as were many others I have come across over the years.

I would also like to acknowledge the Eagle Worldwide Ministry Team, many of whom have caught the prophetic anointing and are living by revelation knowledge. They have worked with me in developing and honing my skills. Specifically, I would like to thank Miguel Simon, my associate pastor, who helped to correlate this work. I also want to thank May McKay, Barbara Bius, Patty Thorpe, my administrative assistant, who helped me put together much of this material, and Vicki Grassick, for her assistance in editing the manuscript. Many thanks and appreciations go to the countless others who have put up with my finicky management style and custom of living by revelation knowledge.

TABLE OF CONTENTS

FOREWORD

When God said, "In the last days I will pour out my Spirit," He certainly included our time, because our sons and daughters of this hour are prophetic. They dream things and they envision trends and events, as well as experience open visions. It wasn't so in past generations like it is today. This is a peculiar time in all of human history. God is revealing His mysteries and secrets. God told Daniel "to shut up the book until the time of the end." Why? I believe this is a unique season when God will give enlightenment and illumination through this present generation that will cause those things that have been shadows and types to take on life and breath. Mysteries will no longer be mysteries. The fullness of time is dawning.

Russ Moyer's new book is aptly titled: *Night Watch: Unlocking Your Destiny Through Dreams and Visions*. He not only moves in a prophetic ministry, but has a mantle on his life to mentor those who dream. God inspires dreams, as Joel declared that He would. He not only defines the dreamers, but He delivers them from the paralysis of feeling strange and misunderstood. They say it takes one to know one.

Russ Moyer clearly communicates his message because he is one. This book certainly will not appeal to everyone in the Body of Christ, but to those it does appeal to it will be like water to the thirsty and rain upon a dry and thirsty land.

John Kilpatrick
Pensacola, Florida

INTRODUCTION

Even since I was saved in 1976, the Lord has revealed to me what He wants me to do, including the why and when, by dreams, visions, and revelation knowledge. I decided to write this book based not on my own understanding but on the prompting of the Lord in a dream. In the fall of 2002, I had a dream that I was walking through the park. I sat down on a bench and a nice man was sitting next to me. I was observing the beautiful city landscape, the high buildings in the distance, the busy traffic on the street, men and women jogging and walking their dogs, when the man next to me asked me if I could teach him how to do that. I didn't know what he was referring to and I said, "How to do what?" He said, "Do what you're doing." When he said that, I looked down at my hands. I had a pad of paper in my hands, and I had drawn on the pad the exact duplicate of the peaceful yet busy city scene. I was surprised because I'm not artistic. In fact, I have little or no natural talent, but I responded, "If I can do it, I can probably teach you how." He smiled, and I woke up.

The interpretation of the dream is rather simple. The Lord was letting me know that He wanted me to teach others how to interpret or understand the revelation they receive. I have been living on revelations and interpretations myself for so many years that it seemed like second nature to me. The Lord has used me to interpret the dreams and visions received by people around the world, so they too can apply the wisdom they receive from the Lord to their daily lives. Today, as never before, revelation knowledge is pouring forth from the throne room of God. It's important that every one of us who are His sheep learn to hear and discern His voice.

I am going to share with you the practical understanding I have, but I want you to know that it is not an exact science. Each one of us has a responsibility to seek the Lord on our own. This book is divided into four sections: I will discuss practical teaching on how to hear the voice of the Lord, principles of interpretation, personal and practical examples, and symbols and meanings.

PART 1

HEARING THE VOICE OF THE LORD

REVELATION, UNDERSTANDING AND WISDOM

That the God of our Lord Jesus Christ, the Father of glory, may give unto you the spirit of wisdom and revelation in the knowledge of Him: the eyes of your understanding being enlightened; that ye may know what is the hope of his calling, and what the riches of the glory of his inheritance in the saints.

EPHESIANS 1:17-18

In this prayer, Paul asked for revelation, understanding and wisdom for the Ephesians. I believe that when the Lord God speaks to man, He speaks to him in revelation, understanding, and wisdom.

Revelation is how we see, how we hear, how we feel. It is the way the message is communicated to us. Sometimes it is a vision, sometimes it is a word, and at other times it is a still small voice. In this chapter, I will be discussing the different aspects of revelation.

Understanding is the knowledge of what He showed us, what He spoke and revealed to us. What good does revelation do if we have no understanding of it and don't know what God wants? The purpose of revelation is to give us direction so that we know the hope of His calling. If all we have is the revelation but we don't understand what it means, then we need to have some way to interpret it. Without the interpretation, which is the understanding, we lack direction to know where to go and what to do.

The third aspect of making that word from God fulfilled, empowered, and directive in our life is to have *wisdom*. We need to have wisdom to know whether the word is for this time or for another season. We also need to have wisdom to know where the voice or revelation came from, because the Lord says we are to test the spirits. I believe we can hear from four different sources: God, man, Satan or an angelic visitation such as Jacob as well as the apostle John in the book of Revelation experienced.

Another important area of interpretation is discerning of spirits. We need to know, we need to hear, we need to see, and then we need to have wisdom to know how to implement this in our life. We also need to know the timing, the way of it, the who, the when, and what to make of it.

REVELATION

The first way that God likes to speak to His children is through the Word. It says in John 1:1-5, "*In the beginning was the Word, and the Word was with God, and the Word was God. The same was in the beginning with God.*" We know that Jesus is the Word. He is the Word made manifest. "*All things were made by him; and without him was not any thing made that was made. In him was life; and the life was the light of men. And the light shineth in darkness; and the darkness comprehended it not.*" He is the Word, and there is revelation in the Word because He is life. So there is life in the Word, and there is light and revelation in the Word. The light shines, giving us direction. He loves to speak to us in the Word, but in order to avoid the trap of opening the Word of God and just reading words, we need to speak to the Holy Spirit, we need to open up the Word of God in a place of fellowship and relationship, and say, "O, Holy Spirit, You are the author of this Word. Will You speak to me here?"

This is one way that He gives us revelation. It is the difference between the *Logos* Word, the written Word, and the *Rhema* Word, which is the Word of direction for man.

The second way that God gives us revelation is in dreams, and the third way is in visions. On the Day of Pentecost, Peter said, *"And it shall come to pass in the last days, saith God, I will pour out of my Spirit upon all flesh: and your sons and daughters shall prophesy, and your young men shall see visions, and your old men shall dream dreams"* (Acts 2:17-18). We are in the last days. We are in the days of great revelation glory and great revelation knowledge being released. This is not limited just to the hierarchy. The biggest barrier that has to come down in the church is the barrier between the clergy and the laity. We are all children of God and every one of us is to hear the voice of the Father. We all need to get the dreams and the visions and the revelation for our own lives.

All through the Word men and women of God have heard the voice of the Lord. He has spoken to His children by His Spirit, and He has said that these would be the times when He would pour out His Spirit on all flesh, and that great revelation would be birthed in this hour. In Job 33:14-15 it says, *"For God speaketh once, yea twice, yet man perceiveth it not. In a dream, in a vision of the night, when deep sleep falleth upon men, in slumberings upon the bed."* He said that God speaks to men in a dream, in a vision of the night when deep sleeps falls upon men, in the slumberings upon the bed. That's one of the times that God speaks to His children, and the way He does it is in a dream or a vision. Now, He tells us the purpose in Job 33:16. *"Then He openeth the ears of men, and sealeth their instruction."* He wants to speak to us in a dream and a vision to give us a revelation so we know where to go, so that we know what to do and where we are headed. This is the way He seals our instruction. Job 33:17 says *"that the reason for this is that He may withdraw man from his* [man's] *purpose, and hide pride from man."* When we talk and we walk in our own purposes, our own plans, and our own dreams, we are walking in our own pride, saying that we know, as opposed to listening to Him speaking. It says in verse 18 that this is what keeps man from the pit, from the snare, and from the hand of the enemy. God speaking keeps man from falling.

The fourth way that He speaks to us is in the still small, voice of God. That still, small voice of God has been heard by everyone who calls Jesus Christ Lord, because the Word of God says that no man can say Jesus is Lord except by the Spirit of God. The Holy Spirit reveals it to us, so we have all heard His still, small voice from time to time. That is the prompting of our conscience. That is that word that we receive in our spirit that we know, that somehow we just know. That still, small voice that just whispers in the quiet of the day, the quiet of our hearts, and the quiet of our minds. We need to know that voice and be sensitive and tuned to that voice.

Then, of course, there is the audible voice. First Samuel 3:1 says, *"And the child Samuel ministered unto the LORD before Eli. And the word of the LORD was precious in those days; there was no open vision."* The Lord spoke to Samuel in the voice of his master, Eli. Samuel got up and began to hear in an audible voice the voice of the master. When he went to Eli, Eli told him that it was the Lord. After he went a few times and he still kept hearing the voice, Eli told Samuel to listen, just the way every one of us needs to listen. It is very important that we go with a humble heart and that when we begin to hear the voice of the Lord, we say, "Your servant is here, Lord. I am listening. Speak to me." We see in verse 9, *"Therefore, Eli said unto Samuel, Go, lie down: and it shall be, if he call thee, that thou shalt say, Speak, LORD; for thy servant heareth.' So Samuel went and lay down in his place."* We need to take that time and go to that quiet place. We need to seek Him in that secret place, and say, "Lord, Your servant hears. Your servant listens. Will you speak to me?" God speaks to us in the audible voice, in the still, small voice, in dreams and visions, and in the Word.

In Luke 4:18-19, the Lord spoke these words taken from the book of Isaiah:

> *The Spirit of the Lord is upon me, because he hath anointed me to preach the gospel to the poor; he hath sent me to heal the brokenhearted, to preach deliverance to the captives, and recovering of sight to the blind, to set at liberty them that are bruised, to preach the acceptable year of the Lord.*

There is such a thing as anointed teaching and anointed speaking of the Word of God. First Peter 4:11 says, "*If any man speak, let him speak as the oracles of God; if any man minister, let him do it as of the ability which God giveth; that God in all things may be glorified through Jesus Christ, to whom be praise and dominion for ever and ever.*" Let us speak and minister to one another as the oracles of God. Anointed teaching can impart direction.Each one of us can receive direction from the Word of God and confirmation as to where the Lord is sending us when there is anointed teaching, preached to us by anointed men of God.

The Lord also speaks to us in feelings and emotions, for we are beings of feeling and emotion. He will speaks to us in various ways. That is the way He brings forth revelation. But revelation by itself is not enough. We need to understand what that revelation means, what it does, and what He is trying to say to us. Therefore, we need the interpretation of that revelation, which is the second phase of hearing the voice of the Lord. First we need the revelation, and then we need to have the interpretation.

UNDERSTANDING

The Lord speaks to me in symbols, in allegories, and in parables. I know that many people receive only the revelation, and they never do receive the understanding. God wants us to have understanding and He wants us to grow. Sometimes it is for us to learn and grow and for us to chew on, to meditate on. Sometimes it is for us to take to the godly counsel in our life and share it with them; they are to help us and enlighten us in that hour. Sometimes we are to bring it to a prophetic voice. Sometimes He sends us as a messenger.

It says in Job 33:23-24, *"If there be a messenger with him, an interpreter, one among a thousand, to shew unto man his uprightness; then he is gracious unto him, and saith, Deliver him from going down to the pit: I have found a ransom."* There are dreamers of dreams, and interpreters of dreams, and a gift of interpretation. I interpret dreams from people all over the world. They fax or e-mail me their dreams and the Lord will reveal to me His purpose. But there is more than one interpretation to every dream, and we need to be open to what the Lord is speaking to our hearts. We need to take our dreams to Him in prayer and ask for that interpretation, that guidance, and that direction. We need to be open to it.

If we are a person who is given to dreams, then we need to get some books on how to interpret those dreams in a godly manner from the Word of God, from Scripture. We need to know the symbols and the signs that are in the Word. For example, there are numbers, and numbers have meaning: One means the beginning, and two means division and separation. Therefore, one vision is the beginning of a vision, and two visions is division. Two visions in the same house will bring division, or separation. Three can be something concerning the Trinity or obedience and conformity. Four would be Kingdom rule and reign, and five would be a work of service unto God: a work of the hands of man for service to God. Six would be sin or flesh or evil. Seven would be completion or rest. Eight would be new beginnings or putting off the old and putting on the new. Nine would be the number for harvest and fruitfulness, and ten would be the number for testing in all things, or temptation. So each of these numbers has a meaning. Eleven would be the last hour. Twelve would be joining or coming together, as two or three coming together in My name, God being in their midst. It is a way of spiritually joining people together. Thirteen would be the number for rebellion. Each of these are coded in the Word, and there are places you can refer to. So when you see numbers in your dreams, they have meaning to God. God coded the whole Bible. God speaks symbolically, in order and in codes. We need to begin to understand what they mean.

Colours also have meaning. Red is the colour for passion and black for sin or ignorance. Brown is a colour meaning no life, or maybe being born again but without the Spirit. The colour purple would be for majesty. Orange would be fire, and gold would be glory. The colour yellow is for spiritual giftings. To put a yellow ribbon out is to welcome somebody home, for example. All these things will have symbolic meaning and they will also have meaning for you. They will speak to you in ways that you understand. You need to get on the same wavelength with Him, because His thoughts are not your thoughts, and His ways are not your ways.

Sometimes the strangest dreams I have are from the Lord. Some of the things I see in my dreams are most unusual but they give me direction and guidance. I live by dreams and visions. We are not to live by bread alone, but by every word that comes from the mouth of God. This is how He speaks and confirms things to me. I don't simply minister at any church or go to some place because somebody invites me. I need a confirmation from God: that it is where He wants me to go, and that it is where He wants me to be, so that when I get there, He will be there to meet me with all His power, and all His majesty, and all His glory. There is an assurance in being in the place He told me to be: I don't have to concern myself with what other people think, or what they may say in that place. There is only one person I have to please, and that's Him. So when people ask me if I will come and minister in their church, or be on their radio or television program, I first seek the Lord, and when I hear from God, I know I am supposed to be in that place. When we don't hear from God, we have a tendency to say "Well, He didn't say no, so it must be yes." No! Yes is yes, and no is no. Also, "not now" does not mean "not ever". His delay is not His denial either. Sometimes He uses traffic lights to talk to me. A red light is stop, a green light is go, and a yellow light is proceed with caution.

WISDOM

He speaks to different people in different ways. We need to develop a relationship with Him so that we understand. There is wisdom that goes with hearing and understanding the voice of the Lord. We need to have wisdom concerning why He gave us that revelation. Most things that God speaks to me are for me to take to prayer. I am an intercessor, so He shows me people and things to pray about and people to pray for.

The second part of wisdom is timing. I am presently walking in revelations I received two, three, or five years ago. They were prophetic words that He spoke to me in the Word, or words that He spoke to me when I was in prayer. No matter which way He revealed it to me, whether a dream, vision, or a prophetic voice, I took it back to Him and I asked, "Is this the right timing?" Certainly it was from God, but if I would have stepped out on that revelation right then, I would have been there before God got there, before I was supposed to be there, before He had everything in place for me there. So it was important to seek Him for the timing once I got the revelation. Then I always had to check the source, because God is a God who confirms His Word. I need to discern the spirits. Do I know it is a godly revelation? Does it match up with the Word of God? Do I get confirmation?

Habakkuk 2:1, 3 says, *"I will stand upon my watch, and set me upon the tower, and will watch to see what he will say unto me...For the vision is yet for an appointed time, but at the end it shall speak, and not lie: though it tarry, wait for it; because it will surely come, it will not tarry."* It appears as though tarry means it would be late. It sounds almost like a contradiction but it is not. It may tarry according to man's timing, but God says it will not tarry. It will be there when He says it will be there. It will be there in His timing. We need revelation and wisdom and understanding. We need all three in order to turn this revelation into something practical that we can walk with, so that we can walk in faith.

We have seen the different ways God reveals His heart to us: through the Word, visions, an audible voice, the still, small voice, through the preaching of the Word, through feelings and emotions, and certainly in the place of prayer. We always need to take the revelation to Him in prayer so that we get understanding, knowledge, and the interpretation of what He has shown us. Then we need to have wisdom to know what the purpose, timing, and source are. We always need to know how to discern these things and put the revelation into operation.

I pray that the Lord would anoint you this day with revelation knowledge. That He would fill you with an understanding of who you are and what you are called to do. That He would birth in you a Kingdom vision and a heart to serve Him and to follow His will and His Word. That you would hear, see, and feel, by the prompting of His Spirit, into the revelatory realm and that you would teach others to soar with you. In Jesus' name, Amen.

KEYS TO UNLOCKING YOUR DESTINY

Revelation
- Revelation serves no purpose without having the understanding.
- Once you have received revelation from the Lord, take it back to Him in prayer to get the understanding, the knowledge, and the interpretation.
- Revelation from the Lord comes to us through various means:
  - The Word.
  - Dreams and visions.
  - His still, small voice.
  - The audible voice of God.
  - Anointed preaching and teaching.
  - Feelings and emotions.

Understanding
- For proper understanding, know that there can be more than one interpretation for every dream.
- Colours and numbers have significant meaning.

Wisdom
- Key aspects of wisdom:
  - Know God's purposes through relationship.
  - Know the timing of His revelation.
  - Check the source of the revelation.

Prayer and Principle

But if they be prophets, and if the word of the LORD be with them, let them now make intercession to the LORD of hosts, that the vessels which are left in the house of the LORD, and in the house of the king of Judah, and at Jerusalem, go not to Babylon.

JEREMIAH 27:18

One of the primary purposes for revelation knowledge is prayer, intercession, and spiritual warfare. It is important for those of us who move in the gift of prophecy or the office of the prophet to know that one of the primary purposes for the revelation we receive is for us to make intercession. Many of us who have a hunger for souls and a desire to see the lost saved get caught up in praying for the harvest rather than for the labourers. In the above scripture the Lord of hosts, who leads the army, wants us to pray for the vessels that are remaining in the House of God. We need to use our gifting for the edification of the body, for the equipping of the saints, and for the work of ministry. We need to understand our spiritual giftings and not just how they operate but what their purpose is and what our responsibility is. It is in that place of understanding our responsibility that we become accountable for our use, abuse, and lack of use of what has been given to us; for to whom much is given, much will be required.

Paul clearly states in 1 Corinthians 12:1, "*Now concerning spiritual gifts, brethren, I would not have you ignorant.*" He doesn't want us to be ignorant. He wants us to be knowledge-able. There are nine signature gifts of the Spirit: the word of wisdom, the word of knowledge, faith, the gift of healing, the working of miracles, prophecy, discerning of spirits, diverse kinds of tongues, and the interpretation of tongues. Others gifts include the gift of helps, hospitality, administration, and so on. In this chapter, I am going to focus on hearing the voice of the Lord, which is part of the revelation gifting and important in the use and operation of the prophetic, the word of knowl-edge, and the word of wisdom.

No matter what we do, every one of us needs to hear the voice of the Lord and we need to hear it for ourself. It is cer-tainly wonderful when we get a prophetic word from a man or woman who is sent by God to minister to us in a prophetic anointing. We certainly need to get the word from an anointed preacher who will preach the Gospel of Jesus Christ and open up our hearts. But first and foremost, we need to know how to hear the voice of the Lord for ourself and know the differ-ent ways that the Lord speaks to us.Ephesians 1:16-18 is the apostolic prayer of Paul. He says,

[I] *cease not to give thanks for you, making mention of you in my prayers; that the God of our Lord Jesus Christ, the Father of glory, may give unto you the spirit of wisdom and revelation in the knowledge of him: the eyes of your understanding being enlightened; that ye may know what is the hope of his calling, and what the riches of the glory of his inheritance in the saints.*

Paul tells us in verse 17 that God's prayer for us is that we may have wisdom, revelation, and knowledge of Him. I be-lieve that in hearing the voice of the Lord, we need to have revelation, wisdom, and understanding or revelation, wisdom and knowledge. The purpose of it is the understanding, as He talks about the eyes of our understanding being enlightened (being able to see, having revelation) for the purpose of knowing the hope of His calling and the riches of the glory of His inheritance in the saints, that we would know, who we are in Him and who He is in us. Another reason why God wants to speak to us is so that we can understand His power, and the power and authority we have in Him as believers. As in Ephesians 1:19-23.

> *"And what is the exceeding greatness of his power to us-ward who believe, according to the working of his mighty power which he wrought, in Christ, when he raised him from the dead, and set him at his own right hand in the heavenly places, far above all principality, and power, and might, and dominion, and every name that is named, not only in this world, but also in that which is to come: and hath put all things under his feet, and gave Him to be the head over all things to the church, which is his body, the fulness of him that filleth all in all."*

According to Paul's prayer, I am going to believe the Lord that He is going to give you revelation, wisdom, and understanding in Him. Every one of us needs to hear the voice of the Lord for ourself because every one of us who is a Christian needs to be obedient.

In this first section, *Hearing the Voice of the Lord*, I am going to share with you the general workings and in the next section, *Principles of Interpretation*, I am going to share with you the very specific parts and the very practical use of hearing the voice of the Lord. For every one of us who call Jesus Christ Saviour, He is more than just our Saviour, He is also our Lord. If He is our Lord then He needs to be our Master, and as a slave obeys his Master, we need to do what the Lord says.

There are a number of ways that we need to know what the Lord speaks. He speaks to us in general terms and then He speaks to us in very specific terms, in a lot of different ways, through a lot of different channels and from a lot of different realms. He speaks to His children. The Word of God says, "*If you love me you will obey my commands.*" In order to obey Him, we have to know His desires. Now certainly the Word of God will give us the commands that He has for Christian living, but there is more to being obedient than just following the commands that are laid out in the Word. There is also the everyday work of hearing the voice of God and seeking His direction.

We are walking in days of revelation glory, and the Word of God says that we need to be led by the Spirit. In all things we need to be led by the Spirit, not just in a few things, not just in big matters, not just in obeying the Ten Commandments. In fact, in the church today, one thing that causes me to reflect is that we have people screaming, "We want the Ten Commandments in the church, we want the Ten Commandments in the schools, we want them in the courts." I want to see the Ten Commandments lived by the people of God! Most people don't even know the Ten Commandments. They can't tell you what they are, so how can they expect to obey them? We need to be led by the Spirit in all things. We need to be guided by the Spirit in all the decisions we make. We need to begin to go to God in every possible way, seeking Him for His guidance and direction. One reason we don't hear the individual direction God gives us is because we are not listening. It is because our prayer life is not what it should be.

If you want to know what your spiritual temperature is, check your prayer life. Check your relationship with Jesus Christ. For most of us, if we spent as much time talking to our spouse every day as we do talking to the Lord, we would have nothing left of a marriage. If your relationship is broken, separated, or nonexistent, then you need to begin right now to put that relationship in order, because the place where God speaks most to His children is in that place of fellowship and communication, in that place of prayer. When we go to prayer, we have to make sure we are expecting to listen.

Many times, our problem when we go to prayer is that we go with a whole shopping list. We go there and pray for a couple of minutes and sometimes we even pray rehearsed or canned prayers, and the next thing you know, we are going through a whole shopping list of everything we want. One of the ways to check the depths of our Christianity is to notice whom we are praying for and what we are praying about. If all of our prayers are about us, what we want, what we are going to do, and everything having to do with and pointing to our needs, then we need a fresh touch of God in our prayer life and in every aspect of our lives.

As we begin to get revived in Christ and we begin to pray what is on His heart, we need to go to Him listening obediently. If we want to hear the voice of the Lord, we need to stop talking when we get there. Most of the time when we go to that secret place, our prayer life is all about bless my brother, bless my cousin, bless my uncle, bless my sister; all we ever talk to Him about is all of our needs. We fail to realize that God already knows all of them.

There is another way to pray. There is a better way: pray from a place of relationship. Begin to speak to Him as you speak to a friend. Open up your heart to Him. Don't worry about sounding and acting all religious. Just open up your heart to God as though He is your best friend, because He is. Go there open to Him, open to hearing. Pray that prayer for yourself that Paul prayed: that God would give you revelation, wisdom, understanding, and the knowledge of Him; that your eyes would be opened. Pray that you would be able to hear, that there would be sensitivity in your hearing, and that your heart would be right and obedient before Him.

We are changed from glory to glory, so we need to get in the glory when we go to pray. Don't just go there with your shopping list of things to pray; He already knows your shopping list. We need to go there and do what we do best. We need to praise Him. The way to get in the glory is to praise Him. Just begin to praise Him. Begin to thank Him.

If you have nothing to thank Him for, then you know you already have a problem with your Christianity because if you are saved, you have plenty to thank Him for. Just begin to give Him thanks. How do we enter His presence? With thanksgiving! We enter into His gates with thanksgiving (see Psalm 100:4). Give Him praise, give Him honour, give Him glory, praise His name. Thank Him for your life, thank Him for your health, thank Him for your salvation, and thank Him for your family. Thank Him even for the things you are expecting and are yet to come. For all that He has done for you in your life, give Him thanks.

Continue to praise Him until the spirit of worship comes, and then worship Him. Worship is different from praise. In worship we get to that new level. When the spirit of worship comes, begin to worship Him for who He is, for He is the God of majesty! Exalt Him and magnify His name! Let Him know how high and lifted up He is in your heart. Let Him know that you know that He is the God that set all the heavens in place, that He has every grain of sand on the beach counted. Give Him honour and glory, and worship His mighty name. Worship Him. He is the King of kings; He is the Lord of lords. He is the Beginning and He is the End. Let Him know that He is the One. Worship Him until the glory comes, which is the manifest presence of God. Just continue to worship Him.

When I begin to praise and worship Him, I know He is there. I don't have to ask Him if He is there because the Word says that He inhabits the praises of His people, so I know He is there. The minute I begin to praise Him, I know He is there. The depth of Him being there is the place that I can get to in worship. He doesn't need worship. He doesn't have an ego problem. I need worship. Why? In order to draw the glory of God to me.

Once I get to that place where the glory is and where I feel His presence, I know He is there. I don't have to tell Him all the things that I need; He already knows. When I get in the glory, as I start worshiping, sometimes I'll lie in His presence or sit in His presence or walk in His presence. Sometimes I just talk to Him from the depths of my heart about my emotions and my feelings. Sometimes I just listen. It is a beautiful place; it is a place of peace. It is a place of fellowship. Sometimes He speaks; sometimes He doesn't have to. His presence in the room says it all. Some of you who are in love with your spouse and have a good relationship with them know that sometimes you can just sit in the same room and nobody has to say anything, for peace and love are made manifest in that place. How wonderful it is to be in fellowship with the Lord Jesus Christ. That's the place where we will hear Him if we will listen to Him.

It's like receiving a phone call from sister Suzie in the morning before she is ready to send the kids off to school. She says, "Oh, it's so important that I called you today. You won't believe what I am going through. You don't know what I am going through with my kids and my husband. I haven't felt good, I couldn't sleep right last night, I'm heading off to work now, and I'm going through so much at that job. By the way, I gotta go. I'll see you later on. Have a nice day." That's what we do to the Lord. That's not fellowship at all. Sister Suzie didn't find out one thing that was on my heart and I found out nothing but the nonsense that was on hers. All she did was take her bucket and dump it on me. I need to be in that place with the Lord that every time I go there and every time I pick up that phone in prayer, I am not just there with a great need. Sometimes I am there to fellowship, sometimes I am there to listen, sometimes to talk and share my emotions and my heart.

Every time is different. Your place of prayer is the number one place to hear from the Lord.

Your prayer life needs to be ongoing. Pray without ceasing, as Paul said. Everywhere we go and everything we do, our life is a prayer, but there are seasons and moments when we need to just set ourselves aside and be in fellowship with the Lord. We need to shut ourselves off from the phone, the kids, the people, and all things and just tune our ears to Him so that we can hear Him in the Spirit. We need to begin to pray and ask the Holy Spirit to speak to us. He loves to speak to His children. That's the purpose of man: to fellowship with God. He didn't need somebody to tend the garden. He doesn't need a barber or a hairdresser or a car salesman. The purpose of man is to fellowship with God, to walk with Him in the oneness and unity of the Spirit in the garden.

Do you want to see all hell break loose? Set ten, fifteen minutes or half an hour aside for prayer. Say you're going to give this time to God and you going to go to this place and pray. When you do that, you will see everything come at you. Thoughts will begin to bombard you from everywhere. Why? Because the enemy knows that that is the critical danger point. It is a place of relationship. It is a place of knowing Him. God said that those who know Him would do great and mighty exploits. That's right. We will do great and mighty exploits if we know Him.

Just because we know about Him doesn't mean that we know Him. We may read about Him in the Bible, but if we don't have a walkie-talkie relationship, then we don't really know Him. We need to know His thoughts and we need to know His ways because they are different from ours. Certainly He needs to know about us, but He already does. So when we go there, lets go there listening as much as we do talking so that we can begin to sensitize our ears, our hearts, and the eyes of our spirit to Him. Then we may see and know and understand what He desires of us.

We need to go to Him seeking revelation, wisdom, understanding, and a knowledge of Him, that the eyes of our understanding would be enlightened. That we would have revelation. Revelation of what? Of the hope of His calling: the direction that He has for us. Not just the general calling of our life, our mission, and our ministry, because every one of us is a minister, but for our everyday needs. We need to begin to seek Him for the little things and the big things, for the small directions and the big directions. We all want to seek Him when it comes to a helpmate, what college to go to, or what church to attend. He wants us to come to Him in all things. He wants us to bring it all to Him in prayer. He wants us to bring it all to Him and let Him give us the guidance and direction we need. He sees it all on the other side. He knows it all. He knows what is going to happen and how and when and where. We need to submit to that and we need to yield to that so we can know the hope of His calling, so we can be obedient, so we can avoid the pitfalls. We end up going from one ditch to the other ditch because we don't have the direction of the Lord. We need to yield. We need to be led by the Spirit even as Paul was led by the Spirit in Acts 16. He wanted to go to one place to preach and then he had the vision of the man of Macedonia. When he saw that vision, he knew he wasn't supposed to go elsewhere. He knew that where he had wanted to go wasn't the place to go.

It is very important that we become sensitive to Him in that place of prayer. Also, as we begin to walk out what He tells us to do, we need to be sensitive to a few other things in order to be led by the Spirit. Once we know it is God and He has given us that direction, we need to be obedient to walk it out. We need to step out in faith. We need to apply our faith to what He tells us to do. In Colossians 3:15 it says. *"Let the peace of God rule in your hearts."* This is one of the ways that we are guided. By the peace in our spirit we can be guided to know that we are on the right track, to know that we have a hold and a grip on God. He will give us that peace in our spirit to let us know that we are headed in the right direction. It is so important that we realize what that peace is, it is very, very important. It says in verse 15, *"And let the peace of God rule in your hearts, to the which also ye are called in one body; and be ye thankful."* This tells us to give thanks, recognize our calling, and let the peace of God rule in our hearts.

Just as surely as the peace of God can rule in our hearts and tell us that we are led by the Spirit in the proper direction, we need to know, as it says in Deuteronomy 32:10-11, that He stirs our nest. We will know by that uneasiness that we are not in the right place. We need to begin to sensitize our spirits. We need to sensitize ourselves in every way. When we go to prayer, we need to pray the prayer that Paul prayed for the Ephesians, so that we know the hope of our calling, so that we know what the riches of the glory of His inheritance is for us. Then we can begin to walk in revelation, wisdom, and understanding, and that is what I pray for you today.

I pray that He will enhance your prayer life and open up a relationship and a fellowship between you and Him; that you will walk together in a place of unity and understanding. I ask that the King of Glory, by His Spirit, will touch your ears and tune them to His voice, and touch your eyes that you would behold His glory. That your eyes would be enlightened. That the eyes of your understanding would be opened. That you would begin to get revelation from the heavenlies. That you would understand what you see and what you hear. That you would go deeper in the knowledge of Him and in the calling He has for you. I pray that He would seal His instruction to you both day and night, in dreams and visions and revelation from the heavenlies and that you would know what He has called you to do and be in Him. I pray in the name that is above every other name, in the name of the Lord Jesus Christ.

May His Spirit dwell richly in you. May you greet one another with great love. May He open you up to the deeper things in Him. That you may soar into heavenly places, in the realms of glory that are in His Spirit, on the wings of worship and praise. May He touch you this day. In Jesus' name, Amen.

Keys to Unlocking Your Destiny

- A primary purpose of revelation is for prayer, intercession, and spiritual warfare.
- Revelation also serves to understand His power, and what power and authority you have as a believer.
- The purpose of revelation for those who walk in the gift of prohecy or in the office of the prophet is primarily for intercession.
- Prayer is about a relationship, not a shopping list.
- We are changed from glory to glory. To get in the glory: Praise Him, and then worship Him until the glory comes.
- Once you receive the revelation and the understanding, you need to be obedient by walking out what the Lord has revealed to you.
- We will all give an account for the use, misuse, and abuse of the revelation given to us.

PART 2

PRINCIPLES OF INTERPRETATION

THE JOURNEY FROM REVELATION TO WISDOM THROUGH UNDERSTANDING

For God speaketh once, yea twice, yet man perceiveth it not. In a dream, in a vision of the night, when deep sleep falleth upon men, in slumberings upon the bed; then He openeth the ears of men, and sealeth their instruction, that he may withdraw man from his purpose, and hide pride from man. He keepeth back his soul from the pit, and his life from perishing by the sword. He is chastened also with pain upon his bed, and the multitude of his bones with strong pain.

JOB 33:14-16

This subject is NOT taught very often in church settings, but it's one of the key ways that God speaks to us. It's certainly one of the key ways throughout the Word that the Lord has spoken to both men and women of old, and it is happening now as it happened then. He is the same yesterday, today, and forever. There's no place in the Bible that says God would stop speaking to His children. In fact, that's the very purpose for which He created man: to fellowship and commune with Him. Certainly, we hear from Him in many different ways: we hear from Him in the Word as a primary way, we hear Him in that still, small voice, and we hear from Him through prophetic voices. As the Lord speaks to us individually, one of the key ways that He likes to speak to us is in dreams and visions. I am going to lay a foundation through Scripture to show that it does happen, why it happens, and what the purpose of dreams and visions is. God wants to give us direction and guidance. He wants to seal direction to us even in the night season.

I was saved in 1976, and about forty or fifty days later, driving along the highway believing the promises of God concerning the baptism of the Holy Spirit, I was baptized sovereignly by the Spirit of God in my car. The power of God filled me in such a strong way that I began to cry, and had to pull over to the side of the road. I lay on the stones, on my face in a suit and tie, and God just overtook me with waves of His glory and His power and His presence. I knew that I had received the promise that Jesus spoke of, the promise of the baptism with fire and power. From that time on, I have never been the same. I was relatively unchurched, raised as a Catholic, but not a staunch churchgoer. Many are good Catholics. I wasn't one of them. I was in a place of desperation where sin had overtaken me. I received Jesus by reading the Word and I received His baptism, sovereignly.

I didn't know any better; nobody told me any different. I didn't have a lot of spiritual consultants like we have walking around in the church today. I knew what I had read, I believed it in my heart, and the Lord showed it to me as just He had done it in the Word. It was simple for me. I knew what to expect according to what Peter said in Acts 2 in that great sermon on the Day of Pentecost. It was the same promise I saw in Joel as well. The promise of the Father came into the Upper Room like a mighty rushing wind and tongues as of fire came to rest on those believers that day. The Lord will do the same for His believers this day!

Acts 2:16-17 says, "*This is that which was spoken by the prophet Joel; and it shall come to pass in the last days, saith God.*" We are in the last days, the clock is ticking, all we need to do is look around. If we have discerning hearts and discerning spirits, we will know that these are the last days that Peter spoke of. God said, *"I will pour out of my Spirit upon all flesh; and your sons and your daughters shall prophesy, and your young men shall see visions, and your old men shall dream dreams: and on my servants and on my handmaidens I will pour out in those days of my Spirit; and they shall prophesy."* That's what Peter preached that day; certainly it came to pass, but he had quoted Joel. We see in Joel 2:28 that this prophetic word includes every single one of us: sons and daughters, old men and young men, guys and girls, bond and free. The promise is for every one of us. This is one of the ways that the Lord said He was going to pour out of His Spirit and speak to His children: in dreams and visions—and He does!

Since I didn't know any better, I believed for it and immediately began to get dreams and visions, even that first day. From that point on, God began to speak to me in dreams and visions and He began to tell me how He was going to start me in business. I had no business experience, no education, and no money, but over the next five or six months He continued to speak to me in dreams and visions and tell me what He was going to do and what I was going to do. I wasn't sure of all the details, but He would show me this wonderful promise that He had for me, a promise that He indeed fulfilled in the years to come! From that point on, I began to learn to hear the voice of God. He began working with me, making it very simple at first and teaching me by the Spirit. I started my business according to dreams and visions. He told me what area of business He wanted me involved in and how to do it. He told me, at times, who to and who not to do business with. He guided my every step. Because I didn't know anything or I didn't know any better, I would wait on Him and pray and believe. I had no other hope but the hope I had in Him. As I began to make progress, He began to speak more to me because I acted on what He gave me. I believed Him and made bold steps of faith into the dreams and visions He was showing me and the promise He had laid on my heart. What a wonderful God we serve. He guided me in business for nearly twenty years. At one time, I had several different security-related businesses and over two hundred employees: Eagle Security, Eagle Systems, and Eagle Monitoring. I did not know at the time that the eagle was symbolic of the prophetic and that this would be my primary calling, but He did!

From the moment the power of God fell on me in the car, I was dramatically and forever changed. There was a new boldness and a new certainty that God was with me. How wonderful to be filled with the Holy Ghost. How wonderful that the Comforter comes and speaks to us. When the Spirit of God comes into our being in that fresh new way, there's an assurance and confirmation that everything Jesus spoke is true. It's the promise of the Father that Jesus spoke of that lets us know He is at the right hand of the Father. There's a new assurance that He would never leave us alone. He said it was better for us that He would go to the Father because He would send the Holy Ghost who would guide and direct us, who would comfort, strengthen, and walk with us. This promise is for everyone. God is not a respecter of persons.

With every revelation comes responsibility. We must be obedient. When we don't move with the prompting of the Spirit who is in us or the conviction in our conscience, we harden our heart and that makes it more difficult for Him to come. If He continues to talk to us and we ignore Him, how long will He contend with us? The more faith you apply to that voice stirring inside of you, the more revelation you will receive and the more you will grow. When we are faithful with what He gives us, He will give us more. I believe that the dream or the vision is the revelation; it's one of many ways that the Lord speaks to us. The message that He tries to convey needs to be a threefold communication with us. It needs to have three separate and distinct parts so that we can understand what God is trying to say and the message can come to fulfillment in our lives.

The first part is revelation: what we see, hear, feel, and experience, what we read and how we discern it. The second part is understanding: the knowledge of what's being spoken. What does the revelation mean? I need to be able to interpret it. The Lord speaks plainly, but even when He walked the earth, He spoke many times in parables. He spoke very symbolically to men and women in the Word. Ezekiel and Daniel, like many of the prophets, saw visions. Some of them saw in allegories and some of them saw in symbols; some of them heard and had to discern in order to interpret what they had received. It is the same way with us: first we need the revelation; second we need the understanding, or knowledge. We need the interpretation of what the revelation means, because if all we have is the revelation, if all we have is the dream, how are we going to know what God means, what He wants us to do, or when He wants us to do it?

It is not a full message until you get the interpretation, and then after the interpretation (after you get the knowledge), you also need the wisdom, and this is the third part. Just as Paul prayed for the Ephesians, we need the Spirit of revelation, the Spirit of knowledge, the Spirit of understanding, and the Spirit of wisdom. We need to know what the revelation means, we need to know the interpretation, and then we need to have wisdom. Let's move forward in wisdom. The Word says that if anyone lacks wisdom let him ask; we have not because we ask not. Every day I ask for more wisdom.

I believe wisdom is threefold. We need to know first how to discern. We are to test the spirits. Is every dream from God? No, just the same way that not every thought is from God. I believe there are four potential origins of any word that comes into our minds. Certainly, it can be from God in dreams and visions, or from the Word, an audible voice, or a still, small voice. Can the enemy speak to us? Yes! He drops things into our minds, so we have to make sure that the voice we're hearing is the voice of God. It can be from self, too. We each have a soul, mind, will, and emotions. These can generate the thoughts and ideas themselves. There are also examples in the Word where angels spoke. I believe there are four possible sources that we can hear from: We can hear from God, we can hear from a demonic source, we can hear from ourselves, or we can hear from a messenger from Heaven, from an angel. Surely as it was then it is now; nothing has changed. The Lord is the same yesterday, today, and forever. He's just doing a new thing today. He's singing a new song. There's a lot more revelation coming forth in this hour: These are times of revelation glory. End-time prophecy is unfolding before our eyes.

Even though we receive revelation, the other part of wisdom comes when we get understanding. We need to discern the origin of the voice, where it came from; and also very importantly, we need to know the timing of the revelation. Not every revelation is for now. We need to know if it is for now or for a future date. Is the revelation that I'm receiving today from God? And is it for now? Is it for later? What is the timing of it? Is it something for me or is it something I see that's for others? I need to mix wisdom, revelation, and understanding. All three of these together then allow me to bring forth a message. God can not only give me a revelation, but He can also then tell me what He wants me to do with it. We see a good example of this in Job 33:14-19,23. It says in Job 33:14 that God speaks once, then twice, yet man perceives it not. God speaks to him in a dream, in a vision of the night when deep sleep falls upon men, in slumberings upon the bed. This is one of the key times that we can hear from God because it's one of the times that our own conscience level, the watchman that stands at the door of our minds, is at rest and God can slip in the instruction that He has for us. In verse 16, God is not talking about the outside; He is talking about the inside, opening the ears of understanding: and He *"sealeth their instruction."* How does He seal our instruction? In a dream, in a vision, when a man is in a deep sleep on his bed, then He opens up the ears of his understanding and seals their instruction. He does this, it says in verse 17, *"that he may withdraw man from his purpose."* God withdraws a man from his own purpose. When we set ourselves on our own purpose, we set ourselves up in a prideful way to listen to our own thoughts. Instead, He said we are to be led by the Spirit. He said that *"the just shall live by his faith."* It also says in verse 17 that He will *"hide pride from man."* God is saying that He will withdraw man from his purpose and hide pride from him. *"He keepeth back his soul from the pit, and his life from perishing by the sword."* We see here in verse 18 that the instructions that come from God are the ones that tell us we're headed toward a pit, we're headed toward a fall, something that could lead us to a place of perishing in our walk, life, and mind by our own will. God wants to help us to avoid the pitfalls of life and live it to its fullest. God will seal the words of instruction to turn a different way and will tell us that we need to make a turn and that we were following the wrong path. Successful men and women are flexible enough to change their direction when they must. The Lord will lead and guide by the dreams and visions that He gives us. According to verse 19, He corrects man in dreams and visions, many times not just to correct our direction but, also when our lives are out of order, if we are living in sin or deception. For example, many times He will tell me about things that are going on in my own life that He wants me to address, issues that I need to deal with. He does all of this in dreams and visions.

Then He continues in verses 23-24 saying, *"If there be a messenger with him, an interpreter, one among a thousand, to show unto man his uprightness; then he is gracious unto him, and saith, Deliver him from going down to the pit: I have found a ransom."* There are also messengers who will interpret. Does that mean that people who get a dream won't interpret? No. I believe that every one of us needs to do some interpreting for ourselves. Certainly other people can help you, as many people have helped me over the years to interpret revelation that God has given me. However, I don't move on the interpretation or revelation of others. I move on the revelation that God gives me, on hearing and understanding the voice of God in my own spirit. I move on the word that God speaks to me personally, not on the revelation or the interpretation of another. I have to know the voice of God for myself! Certainly I take counsel from people who I know have the gift of interpretation and have the understanding and the knowledge, just as I take counsel from anyone who is trained in a specific area of life. When I use my computer, sometimes I need counsel from somebody who knows how to use the computer. Can I do it myself? Would it be better if I did it myself? I can start it up myself and I can get my own e-mail, but as I get into the more complicated aspects of it, I need to find somebody who's more experienced or more knowledgeable in that particular area than I am. I am not so proud that I won't reach out for counsel and help from others when I need it.

At times I'll get the revelation, I'll get the interpretation, and then I'll sit down with the people that God has placed in my life as key people that I go to when I need counsel. When I am seeking advice or direction, I'll go to them and share with them the revelation and the interpretation that I have and we'll discuss the wisdom of it. We will try to recognize what God is trying to tell me and the timing of it. Whether it's for me to move, whether it's for me to go, whether it's for me to pray, they'll help me with the wisdom side of it. God does send godly counsel into your life and He also speaks to His children in dreams and visions as He spoke to Ezekiel, as He spoke to Isaiah, as He spoke to Joseph, as He spoke to Daniel, as He spoke to Peter, and as He spoke to Paul. When Paul was headed in the wrong direction and he received the Macedonian vision, that changed and altered his course and allowed him to go another way. When Peter wanted to preach to the Jews only, God revealed to him that now was the hour that the Gentiles were also to receive the message; things that He called clean were to be considered clean. God revealed this to him in a vision. God loves to speak to His children in dreams and visions. He did then, He does now, and He will continue to do so. There will be an increase of revelation knowledge coming from the throne the closer we get to that moment when Jesus comes out of Heaven on His white horse with a sceptre of iron, fire in His eyes, and a whole army with Him. As we wait for the Second Coming of the Lord Jesus Christ, know that revelation knowledge is being poured forth from the throne. God is speaking to His children and He is guiding them through dreams and visions.

Heavenly Father, I could never thank you enough for the prophetic anointing and the gift of prophecy. By the power of the Holy Spirit and in the name of Jesus Christ, I proclaim a release of revelation knowledge over the hearts and the lives of my brothers and sisters. Father, that you would release them into a new realm of revelation. That You would begin in their heart that journey, step by step, day by day. That you would reveal to them their destiny. That you would reveal Your purpose and Your plan for their lives. That You would bless them with revelation, wisdom and understanding, in the name of the Lord. In Jesus' name. Amen.

KEYS TO UNLOCKING YOUR DESTINY

If anyone lacks wisdom, let him ask.
To interpreting the message I need wisdom:
Wisdom to know who it is from:
- Is it from God?
- Is it from me?
- Is it from man?
- Is if from the devil?

Wisdom to know who it is for:
- Is it for me?
- Is it for someone else?
- Is it for the church?

Wisdom to know what to do with it:
- Pray
- Prophesy
- Alter my course of action

Wisdom to know when:
- Is it for now?
- Is it for a time yet to come?

We need God's wisdom to answer all the questions.

PRACTICAL APPLICATION: WRITING THE VISION

*I will stand upon my watch, and set me upon the tower,
and will watch to see what he will say unto me, and what
I shall answer when I am reproved. And the LORD
answered me, and said, Write the vision, and make it
plain upon tables, that he may run that readeth it. For
the vision is yet for an appointed time, but at the end it
shall speak, and not lie: though it tarry, wait for it;
because it will surely come, it will not tarry.*
HABAKKUK 2:1-3

The Word says in Habakkuk 2:14, *"For the earth shall be filled
with the knowledge of the glory of the LORD, as the waters
cover the sea."* These are times of revelation glory, when God
is releasing revelation knowledge like never before to and
through His children. He's raising up prophetic voices all over
the earth, a whole generation that will speak forth the Word of
God and the heart of God. He's pouring out His Spirit on all
flesh and the knowledge of the glory of the Lord shall cover
the earth as the waters cover the sea. Hallelujah!

In the last chapter I spoke about some of the foundations in
the Word, about why and how we hear from God in dreams
and visions, and how this has been documented in the Word.
In this chapter, I'm going to touch on the practical aspect of

dreams and visions as I share from the book of Habakkuk. I'm going to share practical applications and steps that I take in the area of dreams and visions, how I get the revelation and what I do with it from there.

In these days revelation glory is being released in all the earth. I live by dreams and visions and by prophetic utterances. That's the way I come, that's the way I go, that's the way I turn, and that's the way I stop. I am not the type of person who just shows up if I am called to minister at a church or in some other setting. When someone calls me to come and minister, I say to that individual that I will pray with them and that we will see what God says. Then I wait on the Lord until I hear from Him about whether or not to go. This way, when I get there, I know that I'm in the place where He told me to be so I will have the authority and power that I need. I know that if He has sent me, He'll take care of me and He'll help me to do whatever I need to do there. I don't have to worry, and when I get there I won't have to impress anybody. I don't want to be the person who just showed up; I want to be the person who was sent! There's something big about being the man or woman sent by God. I believe God is looking for those He can send and those He can tell not to go, those who will go and come and stop and turn whenever He says. That's what revelation glory is all about: being led by the Spirit. He said that His children would be led by the Spirit, and these are days when we need to be led by the Spirit.

There are a lot of people who hear from God. He speaks to His children in very different ways and at many different times. These are practical aspects of how God shares with me, how He directs me, and how He guides me. But you need to develop a relationship with Him yourself, because it is in the place of relationship that you will understand His vocabulary and the way that He speaks to you. I'm also going to share with you some of the prophetic ways God speaks and symbols that He uses when He talks to us.

In this chapter I want you to know some practical steps that I take. I pray continually as Paul said. I pray everywhere I go and I try to make my life a prayer unto the Lord. I try to stay in prayer, I try to stay in the posture of prayer, and I try to stay in the Spirit and not in the flesh. I try to walk in the place where I'm one step away from the voice of the Lord. I remain open to him, open to hear Him, and open to speak His Word all the time. I want to be ready in season and out of season. In addition to just praying wherever I go, there are times in my day I go to pray. Times that I set aside for just Him. Times when I try to close off the rest of the world. When I go to stand my watch, when I go to that secret place, that quiet place in Him, when I go and stand beneath the wings of the Most High God, when I sit at the feet of the Lord at the throne, when I go and just wait on Him, worship Him, and praise Him, I want to go prepared.

First of all, I want to go expecting, because anything we receive from God, we receive by faith. I also go not expecting a one-sided conversation: I go expecting to hear from Him. I hear from Him every time I go and I like to stay until I get what I was looking for. I go to prayer and shut out the whole world. I shut the phones down and close the doors. I quiet myself and turn myself away from my own thoughts, my own ideas of the day, and from all the outside influences that might distract me and take me away from the things of God. When I go to that place where I praise and where I worship Him, when I go to that place of solitude and oneness in Him; when I go to my secret place with Him: that place of fellowship in the cool of the day, to sup and drink of Him, He pours Himself out and into me. He's my Father, my friend, the lover of my soul.

I love to minister. I love to minister to God's children, and I love to pray with them. I love intercessory prayer and prayer meetings, places where I go for corporate worship and corporate prayer but more than anything else, I like that quiet, secret time I spend with God. The time when it's just Him and me is the most exciting time of my whole day; it's the most exciting aspect of my whole life. It's about Him and me: He Who made me and loves me, He who knew me before I knew me, He who knew me before anyone else came to know me in a way that only He can know me, and I can know Him in that place of knowing one another, of fellowship and oneness with one another. When I go there, I go very expectant. I go there not to have a one-sided conversation about everything that I want, but I go there open. I speak a little, I praise a little, I worship a little, and I listen a lot. I want to go there and listen more than I want to go there and talk. I want to go there expecting to hear from God, looking for direction and guidance, because He wants to give it. He's the General, and the General always wants the Private to know where to go and what to do. He wants to speak to us, so when I go to my secret place with a pen and a pad and a Bible and anything else that I might need, I go there prepared, prepared to stay a while because I usually don't know how long I'll be gone. I don't set aside half an hour to be with God, I just go to be with God and I come out when coming out seems good and feels good to me. It may sound a little selfish, but I like to be with God, and I go there and I stay until I feel the release to leave or until I receive what I was intending to receive.

I like what Habakkuk said in chapter 2 verse 1, *"I will stand upon my watch, and set me upon the tower, and will watch to see what he will say unto me."* He said he would stand upon his watch, meaning he was going to take time to be with God, and he would set himself upon the tower. God is not going to take you aside and separate you like that. You need to make that commitment to relationship, and that's what Habakkuk was saying. Then he said he would wait and watch to see what He would say to him. Habakkuk was a visionary. I believe that Habakkuk was a man who walked by faith, who received visions and dreams, and who spoke of visions. In fact, that is what he was speaking about in verse 2: *"And the LORD answered me, and said, Write the vision, and make plain upon tables, that he may run that readeth it."* When you receive a revelation—when you get a word, if you hear something, if you see something, if you experience something from God—you should write it down. Why? So you can make it plain, so you can pray it in, so you can grab hold of the vision and run with the vision. Sometimes the vision He gives you is a vision for others. But even if it is only for you, write it down so that you can bring it back to God and seek God for more definition and more direction and more expansion of the vision. Record it, prepare yourself, believe into it, and meditate on it. You need to run with it. You need to do something with it.

Habakkuk wasn't planning on just getting a vision and going about his business. He was getting visions so that he could take the vision and run with it. What are you doing with what He has already given you? What are you doing with the vision He has already laid on your heart? Someone will tell me that they received a vision in their spirit from God that He was going to make them an evangelist, so I say, well, get up and do something with it. Write it down, make it plain, and begin to implement it. You'll be surprised how much more you will receive from God when you do something with what He's already given you. If all you're doing is receiving, and you are not doing any giving, why should He give you any more until He sees what you've done with what He has already given you? You need to be realistic. If God gave you a vision, He gave it to you with a purpose. You need to implement it: It's by faith, by stepping out in faith. It says in verse 3: *"For the vision is yet for an appointed time, but at the end it shall speak."* You need to have faith in it: It's going to speak, it's going to be fulfilled. *"It will not lie: though it tarry, wait for it; be-*

cause it will surely come, it will not tarry." This looks like a contradiction, but Habakkuk was saying it may tarry in the eyes of man, but the plan of God will be fulfilled in His perfect timing. God has a special timing for everything. It will not tarry, because He's the on-time God every time, and you need to have wisdom as to the timing of God as well as the vision of God. You need to know what the vision is and you need to be able to interpret what the vision said. You need to use wisdom and turn that vision into the right timing of God. Verse 4 says, *"Behold, his soul which is lifted up is not upright in him: but the just shall live by his faith."* He's telling us we need to take hold of the vision, implement our faith, and apply our faith to the vision so that the vision can be fulfilled, because the just shall live by faith. The just shall live by faith, walk by faith, and be led by the Spirit and not by the flesh. When I go to sleep at night, I go to sleep whenever I can with a tablet next to my bed because I'm expecting to hear from God. A man once said to me, "You can't get a dream every day; don't tell me you get a dream every day?" And I said, "No, on bad days I get a dream; on good days I get lots of dreams." I told him that I live by them!

Someone may call and ask us to speak at their conference and we will say that it's an open door and we will walk through it. Other times we'll say we will pray about it and then we pray a couple of days and don't hear anything. So we call back and say, "The Lord didn't tell me not to go, so I'm going." Just as surely as He knows how to say yes, He knows how to say no; and as surely as He knows how to say no, He knows how to say yes. If He doesn't want you to go, He will tell you. If He wants you to go, He will tell you that too. I make it a point to try to go only where I'm told to go. I'm only going where I'm sent. I'm not saying that I don't ever make mistakes as I try to interpret, but the people who walk in the flesh and walk in the natural make a few mistakes too and go through the wrong doors now and then as well. The stops and the goes are not mine; they're His. I try to discern them. I need to interpret His time and His movement, His lefts and rights. I want to know when He's the One who says to go. I also want to be there at the right time, so I need to discern the things of the Spirit. I want to lean on Him, I want to wait on Him, and I want to spend time in His presence, so I go there with my pad and pen. If I get a dream or a vision, I write it down very specifically.

When writing down a dream or a vision, or what I heard, I get as specific as I can. I want to write every colour. If I see a clock, I write down what time it was. If I hear a number, I want to write down the number. If I see a car, I want to know the colour of the car, the type of the car, and model of the car. If I see a license plate, I want to know the numbers on it. A lot of times when we get a dream, we'll say that we will write it down in the morning. By the time you wake up in the morning, you will have forgotten your dream. I get up and write it down, right then and there while it's fresh in my mind. I'll take a minute and ask the Lord to expound on it, to complete it in my spirit, and I'll pray to Him to tell me if there is anything else I need to know as I begin to write it out. I'll ask the Holy Spirit to bring it back to my remembrance, and then I get as specific as possible about the revelation. I usually also record the time, the date, and the location where I had the dream so that I can have a record of it, because numbers and dates are important. If I see a tree, I want to be able to describe it. In addition to just the specifics of what I saw and what I heard, I also want to write down my emotions. In a dream, if I'm running and somebody is chasing me and I'm scared, I need to write down that emotion because that emotion will also speak to me. It will help me to determine whether something seemed good or bad to me because what I see can be good or it can be bad. Objects (nouns) are things that can be either good or bad in a dream, and there is usually a good and a bad interpretation. I need to write down all my emotions so that I can determine whether it was good or whether I thought it was bad. I want to be as specific as I possibly can. I will know the most about the dream right at that moment; as time passes, so does my memory. So I want to be as specific as I can, write as much as I can, and then I want to go to the interpretation as soon as I have the time.

I interpret dreams for people all over the country and even in other nations. When people send me their dreams to interpret or to help them with those dreams, I always try to tell them not to rely on my interpretation only. They need to take it back to God, they need to get it into their spirit and see what God is saying to them. I can give them some parameters and ideas and I can tell to them what I think, but like anything else, there can be more than one interpretation of any revelation. In fact, when they get a revelation, normally there's an interpretation for me. Then there is a larger revelation that's probably for some other people in my life, and then there's probably a grand revelation that has something to do, many times, with the church at large or a large assembly or group.

I will even preach from time to time right from the revelation that I received in a dream or a vision; I'll minister from that revelation. I received a wonderful revelation when I was in Orlando, Florida. I was ministering at a Carlos Annacondia crusade with Joan Gieson and we were praying for the sick. In between services, I was lying on my bed, just relaxing and resting, when I saw a wonderful vision. In the vision, I saw a judge's bench; it was a real long judge's bench. I was in a room that was paneled with mahogany. It was beautiful. I knew it was somewhere important. From behind the judge's bench, I saw these midgets come out. All the midgets had really big heads, and their faces were the faces of Supreme Court justices'. I saw Kennedy, Souter, and O'Connor's faces very clearly. They were handcuffed to one another as they came out from behind the bench. After the dream, I said what I usually say when I get a revelation: "Lord, what does this all mean?" I began to pray to Him and say, "Lord, what do You mean by this vision? What are You trying to tell me?" You see, we have not because we ask not. I ask when I get a revelation from God; I ask Him what He means and I seek Him. I know that He is a rewarder of those who diligently seek Him. I asked Him what it was all about and why they were Supreme Court justices. He said that when we judge one another, it's about judgment. I asked why they were midgets, and He said that when we judge one another, we stunt our own growth and we put ourselves in bondage to one another. That's why they were handcuffed together. I asked Him why they had big heads, and He said that the root of judging is pride. Then He brought me to the Word in Matthew 7:1, where it says, *Judge not, that ye be not judged.* I've preached in a lot of churches from this revelation. He does that with me a lot: He will give me a revelation and He will take me to the Word; then, as He ministers to me, I take it and I minister right from that revelation. He confirms His Word, not mine. I bring it as accusation and judgment, and preach a message of forgiveness and openness.

I receive a lot of revelation that concerns direction, where to go and what to do. Sometimes, other people get the revelation for me and I get the interpretation. I pray that interpretation in and I pray for the wisdom and timing of it, to make sure I'm in the right timing. Sometimes in dreams, the Lord will show me a lot of different faces and I'll know that they're places I'll be going to in the future. I remember I was at a church in Newmarket, Ontario and a lady who was ministering to me said that she felt I was going to go to Nashville, Tennessee, that somebody was going to pour their life into me. The Lord had already spoken something to me about Nashville in a dream that didn't make sense to me, but I held onto it, wrote it down, prayed into it, and knew that someday I would go Nashville. Well, she released that word over me, and when I got home there was a message on my answering machine from a man not far from Nashville, Tennessee, inviting me to come to Nashville. He and his wife were praying and felt that I was supposed to come. They wanted to minister to me and then wanted me to minister to their people. They wanted to spend the first day just pouring into me. He is a deliverance minister by the name of Roger Miller. He had set up and taught a lot of other ministers and he wanted me to minister to his deliverance ministers. Roger and his wife, Donna, poured into me the anointing and the power that they had in their lives. I knew I was supposed to go because God had spoken it to me. He confirmed His words through a prophetic utterance, and when it happened, I knew I was where I was supposed to be and that it was the right timing.

These are some fundamentals on interpretation and revelation and how to go and seek. In the next chapter, I will be getting into deeper interpretation. Write your visions down. Write your dreams down and begin to pray into them. Be one who diligently seeks Him, because first we have to know that God is, and then we have to know that He is a rewarder of those diligently who seek Him! Let's join our hearts together and believe right now in the One who is the rewarder of those who diligently seek Him, the Lord our God.

I believe that He will begin to give you dreams, visions and heavenly revelation and the prophetic gift. I release you into the revelatory realm of the Spirit. In Jesus' name, Amen.

KEYS TO UNLOCKING YOUR DESTINY

- Seek Him.
- Spend quality time alone with Him.
- Believe Him.
- Go with an expectation of revelation.
- Write the vision.
- Make it plain (with detail).
- Run with it (obey and act).
- Wait on Him.
- Wait on the vision.
- Stand in faith because He is faithful.

DEEPER INTO INTERPRETATION

If there be a messenger with him, an interpreter, one among a thousand, to show unto man his uprightness; then he is gracious unto him, and saith, Deliver him from going down to the pit: I have found a ransom.
JOB 33:23-24

In the last chapter, we talked about writing the vision down and making it plain, standing on our watch, how to get the vision, and what to do with it when we go expecting and believing. Now, with respect to dreams and visions, every single one of them is different and it's very important that we pray, and it's certainly important that we get the revelation for ourselves. There can be more than one interpretation of the same revelation and both can be true: I can get multiple interpretations of the same revelation that will first minister to me, then to a larger group, and then to the church at large. It's very important that we hear from God to determine His timing and what He is trying to tell us. Remember that you need to write down your dream or vision and whether you thought something was good or bad. You need to write down each colour, the times and the numbers that you see, and any emotions that you feel in the revelation, because all of this will factor into the interpretation.

Normally, in the beginning of a dream or in the beginning of the revelation, God will give you the "nouns" that are involved: the *what's*, and the *who's*: who was in the dream and who they could represent in real life. For example, when I see a child, it could be my child or it could be me. If I see myself, it could be me or someone who's in the same occupation. If I see a friend, that friend could be me or it could be the friend himself or even the Holy Spirit. If my friend has red hair, it could be someone else that I know with red hair. If my friend is a hairdresser, that revelation could be for another hairdresser or someone who has a like occupation. If I see a minister, it could be the minister himself or another minister who has a similar-style ministry. Let's say I saw a man like Benny Hinn in a dream; it could represent Benny Hinn himself, or it could represent someone with a healing ministry, or it could be that I'll be involved in a healing ministry and the revelation could be for me. So I need to pray into that revelation.

Normally, in the beginning of the revelation, He will show me the players. Then He will get into the nouns, then the verbs; then He'll tell me the *why's*, the *how's*, and the *where's*. He will let me know what is going on, what's happening in the revelation, and then He'll get into the meat of the message. Other times, He'll give me some timing with it, as we get near the end, and then what to do with it and the wisdom that goes with it. Sometimes it may seem incoherent, but I write it all down. I write it out as plainly, as clearly and specifically, and in as much detail as I possibly can because each of the things I see, hear, or feel or experience will play into the interpretation. The more information I have, the more likely I will get a proper interpretation, so I want to write all the information down.

As we get into the symbolic portions of what the dream means, there are a lot of different symbols that need to be clarified. For a comprehensive list of symbols and their meanings, please refer to the Dream Symbols section of this book. For example, if I see my mother in the dream, it could be my mother herself or it could be someone who was a mother in the faith to me. It could be a mother in the faith in general, or it could be my source, or my church. So, prophetically speaking, a mother can represent a lot of different things.

The revelations you receive are so important that they will be worth seeking God on and spending the time necessary to get the proper interpretation. Once you begin to receive revelations in dreams and visions, you are going to want to begin to get some knowledge about them. I'm going to share with you some symbols of things that I see in my dreams to help you get a good understanding.

Let's start with vehicles. If I see a bicycle, then I know it's a work of man because it requires man's energy and effort for it to happen. If I see bicycle built for two, then it's probably a joint work where I'm joining with someone else in a work. If I see a bicycle built for two and I'm on the back but nobody's sitting in the front, then I know that the Holy Ghost is steering. If I'm in a car, in the passenger seat, and nobody's in the driver's seat, then I know that the Holy Ghost is with me. I know whether it's the Holy Ghost or another kind of spirit by the nature of the dream; by the application of the dream. If I see a boat, that's usually a small ministry or work, and if it's a rowboat, then it's probably a work of man. If I see a motor on the rowboat, I know that we are putting some Spirit with it. If I see a ferryboat, I know it carries a lot of different ministries because the ferryboat carries a lot of passengers and also carries other vehicles, which could represent other ministries. If I see a building and I see a small house, I know it's probably an individual ministry. If it's a shopping center or mall, it's probably a place where you can go where more than one ministry can be in the same place. If I see an apartment building that has both businesses and residences, then I know it's probably a big church or a big ministry that has other ministries attached to it or involved in it along with other individuals, all intermixed. If I see a church, then it probably means a religious work of some sort. It could be the church I'm going to or it could be the church at large. So as I see different things, I need to discern the meaning of what I'm seeing.

With respect to colours, red is a colour for passion or zeal or enthusiasm, but it can also be for rebellion. If I see something red and wild, I usually can recognize some rebellion. But it does not mean everybody with red hair is rebellious. If I see something real dark, real black, if I see somebody all dressed in black, with a dark face and dark hair, then I get a demonic feeling with it. I have to be aware of all the feelings that I sense in a dream. That's why it's important to consider each and every one of these nuances. There are different situations and different circumstances. The colour white usually represents purity and cleanliness. The colour blue is usually divine revelation or spiritual visitation. Yellow usually means gifts of the Spirit. If I see a yellow rose, it means a gift coming to me. A red rose probably means love or passion. If I see a yellow ribbon and it's hung on a mailbox, it probably means I'm welcoming somebody home. The Lord knows how to speak symbolically to us in dreams. If I see purple, it is usually something majestic. If I see black, it can usually means something carnal or sinful. If I see pink, it usually means flesh to me. However, if I see pink and red and blue and yellow, it usually means the glory in the different colours. It would give me ideas of what type of glory or what type of revelation I'm into. When I see a bridge, a lot of times it means a walk of faith; if I see an unsteady bridge or a bridge for one, I know I'm going to take a walk of faith myself and it's going to be a rocky walk. Water has a lot of different meanings: Water can be refreshing, but if I'm in a flood, that can be good or bad. Every one of these revelations has a good or bad interpretation. If I see water and it's clear and pure and I'm sitting looking into the water, it probably means clear revelation or something on a clear day; something pure, something clean, something refreshing. If I see floodwaters, it probably means I'm going to be flooded by something, overtaken by something, or something is trying to overtake me. If I see muddy waters, it's probably something dirty, something hard to see through, something impure. These are just some ideas, and you need to pray into these and work them through. Experiment with these in your own revelation and wisdom and understanding of God.

Numbers in dreams are very important. One is something beginning and two is division or discernment, as in two visions being divide, subdivide or discern or try to understand. Three would be the Trinity, obedience, or conformity. Four is Kingdom rule and reign. Five would be a work of service. If it's in a positive vein, five would be a godly work of service; if it's negative, it could be bondage or a work of man. The meanings of the numbers eleven through nineteen are the reverse of the meaning of the numbers from one through nine. They are the opposite of the result of the application of the base numbers. For example, three means to *"conform"*. The opposite of conforming, and the result of forced conformity, is rebellion. Therefore, thirteen means to *"rebel"*. When a base number is multiplied by ten (*ten* is the measure for the purpose of accepting or rejecting), you must couple the key word of the base number with the thought of acceptance or rejection. For example, the date 5/5/50 means "service accepted" (or "rejected," as the case may be). Five means to *"serve,* ten means to *"measure for the purpose of accepting or rejecting"*, *"testing"* or *"temptation"*; therefore, five times ten equals *"service accepted/rejected"*. One hundred means the fullness of something beginning. If I see three hundred, it would be the fullness of obedience or conformity. A thousand would be the number for maturity. The larger the number, the larger or broader the scope of its application. These are only a few examples of the symbolic meanings of numbers. For a more comprehensive listing of numbers and their interpretations, please refer to the Numbers section of this book.

I had a dream of a 1955 Chevy one day; it was an old car that I once owned. God was trying to tell me that nineteen had to do with unfruitfulness, and He was trying to show me an old work that was trying to come back and visit on me. Because I had an old 1955 Chevy, He showed me an old work, and it was an unfruitful work in that time and season. It was the fullness of an unfruitful work of service unto myself.

I had a vision of the White House a number of years ago. In it I saw a broom sweeping under the edge of the kitchen cabinets, and there was nobody on the broom—the broom was sweeping by itself. I knew there was a spirit on the broom because there was no person sweeping with it, and I knew that it was a good thing. I knew that God was doing the work of cleaning out, cleaning the heart of the White House, because the kitchen is the place of the heart. All the rooms in a house have different meanings. A family room has to do with something being revealed; your family room would be a personal place, a familiar place, a casual place. Your kitchen would be a place of the heart; your bedroom would be a place of intimacy; your basement or attic could be a place where you have something up. When I see a roof, I usually think of a covering, the same idea as with an umbrella, a hat, or a coat representing something that's your covering. When I see hands, it has to do with work; when I see feet, it has to do with my walk. My shoes have to do with being shod with the Gospel or that my feet are being prepared to carry forth the Gospel message. These are all different aspects of dreams and interpretations. If I saw that same broom that was sweeping under the kitchen cabinets in the White House flying across the room, and there was nobody on the broom, it probably wouldn't be the Holy Ghost on the broom. It would probably be some other kind of spirit, like a witchcraft spirit. When the

Lord first started to speak to me, He had to explain the whole dream to me. But the more He talks to me, the quicker I am to understand what He is saying because now we have a better way of communicating with one another. For example, if you were to hire a secretary to work in your office and you wanted her to make a bank deposit the first day on the job, you would have to tell her where the cheques were located, where the deposit slips were and how to fill them out, and how to get to the bank. After she had been working in your office for three months, you wouldn't need to give her all that information again. All you would have to do is ask her to make a bank deposit and she would know how to do the rest. As you begin to develop better lines of communication, you acquire more understanding. The visions can be a little quicker and you can learn more and know more in a quick vision. That's the way it has been with me as I have progressed in this relationship with the Lord.

We need to start learning how to hear the voice of God, and once we hear His voice and understand what He is trying to say to us, we need to have wisdom, discernment, knowledge, and understanding. We need to get into that place of fellowship and oneness with God so we can begin to walk in this revelation. Almost every Christian I meet wants to be obedient in his or her heart. They are really trying to do good for God, but they need a little more teaching and a little more training so they can begin to know what God is trying to speak to them, because the Lord *is* trying to speak to them. Sometimes we just need to have ears to hear.

I want to end this chapter with a prayer for you. I want to see you move in this revelation glory. It's my prayer for you to have wisdom and discernment and knowledge and understanding. Heavenly Father, I ask you now in Jesus' name to cover my brothers and sisters with His precious blood, His lifesaving blood, His wonder working blood. And by Your Spirit, I ask that You would anoint them this day, quicken them as they go, guide them and lead them, direct them and protect them by Your Spirit. Let the prophetic anointing be imparted this day! Let them receive revelation knowledge even in dreams and visions. Father, speak to Your children even now, in Jesus' name. Amen.

Keys to Unlocking Your Destiny

- Vehicles, buildings, and vessels all mean "ministries or lives".
- The size of the vessel is equivalent to the size of the work.
- When powered by man, it usually means "works of the flesh".
- A motor means "powered by an outside source (good or evil)".
- Flying means "getting in the spirit".
- Your personal understanding and life experiences bring personal insight.
- A person who looks like someone or who has the same name, initials, or occupation can mean that person.
- Your old house can mean "your old ministry or life".
- Each room has different meanings, symbolically.
- Regularly read and refer to the Numbers and Symbols sections of this book. It will increase your vocabulary. The Lord knows where you are looking for information and He will honour that.

SEXUAL REVELATION AND INTERPRETATION

Many times in my conversations with individuals who have received revelation from the Lord and are in need of some sort of interpretation, the revelation they receive is sexual in nature, and they immediately discount it as not being from God, but that simply is not so.

First, I usually share with them that sexuality in the context of the marriage covenant is a tremendous gift from God to man. The essence of our sexuality is certainly reproductive in nature, but it is also a joyful and natural experience and expression of our humanity. However, as is the case with most things that the Lord creates, the enemy tries to counterfeit or pervert it for his purposes.

Secondly, our God is not naive, and He certainly is omnipresent. Consequently, He sees all things and is everywhere at once and knows both the good and the bad. The rain falls on the good and evil alike. He certainly is not pleased with the perverted sexual activity that is so prevalent in our society today. I have found Him to be, beyond a doubt, the most intriguing and most all—encompassing personality and mentality imaginable to man— beyond our description. He is an awesome God who knows all things and sees all things. In many cases He uses sexual expressions, both good and evil, to communicate with us. One of the most likely purposes and interpretations that He uses when expressing through sexual activity is in the area of covenant. Sexuality, in the context of marriage, is the consummation of the covenant relationship at its deepest level. So when we see good and natural sexual activity in a dream, many times He is trying to describe a positive covenant relationship.

When the revelation is directed toward a minister or pastor, this could possibly be interpreted as an example of something between him and his congregation, his leaders or team, or a specific individual with whom he has a deeper covenant relationship. It can also be interpreted in the natural with respect to his marital covenant. If it involves a relationship with a businessperson, it could be between him and his business or career, his employer or employee, or a partner and friend within his network or scope. Of course, there is also the natural interpretation.

Now, let's assume that the Lord wanted to speak to us and possibly bring forth warning concerning an ungodly or unfruitful covenant. He may use seduction, fornication, homosexuality, rape or self-gratification to bring forth this warning or correction concerning a potentially dangerous or damaging relationship.

SEDUCTION

If a person in a dream reveals their private parts and you have a negative feeling or emotion about it, it could be a warning of an impending attack of the spirits of lust and seduction. This seduction can also be a form of manipulation and control, which is a form of witchcraft.

NAKEDNESS

Nakedness and nudity can also appear to be quite natural in a dream and not negative at all. In these cases it means innocence, vulnerability, liberty, and the like.

FORNICATION

I have never had fornication in a dream to be a positive thing. It normally indicates a relationship outside of the boundaries of covenant, or wanting to experience intimacy without responsibility or commitment.

ORAL SEX

Many times oral sex will relate to ungodly words spoken or vows made that will not be fulfilled or fruitful.

HOMOSEXUALITY

Homosexuality is an ungodly covenant relationship that the Lord detests and calls an abomination. Homosexuality can also, at times, mean the fruit of rebellion and disobedience.

RAPE

At times, rape can be interpreted as domination or forcing your will upon others or having their will forced upon you. It can symbolize forced servitude, bondage, and helplessness. It can be used of the Lord as a form of warning or direction.

MASTURBATION

At times, this can be used symbolically to mean "selfishness, pleasing oneself, pridefulness, or wasting your valuable seed", as in "casting your pearl before swine". In his wonderful book *End Time Warriors*, Apostle John Kelly of the International Coalition of Apostles (ICA), a former athlete, educator, businessman, and a truly powerful man of God, speaks of the vision that he received from the Lord that included masturbation. At first, he rejected it, but the Lord continued to bring it, to fully express His dissatisfaction with certain segments of the Army of God and how they were not reproducing. He said, "God what is this foul, sexual thing I'm seeing?" The Lord answered him and said, "It's none of that. Get your mind out of that place. That's not what I'm talking about. What you are seeing are men and women in ministry wasting the seed of My anointing by not producing spiritual sons and daughters. Yes, they preach, prophesy, and exercise spiritual gifts over My people, but they are not building into My people. They are wasteful! Doesn't the Word speak of My incorruptible seed and the corruptible seed? What I am showing you is that My incorruptible seed can be corrupted by the wasteful use or dissipation of My anointing."[1]

I am not stating that every sexual or violent dream is from the Lord, nor that every good dream is from the Lord. A very important part of our interpretation is that first and foremost we need to seek God concerning the source. He tells us to test the spirits. If you are prone to or have had repeated dreams that are more in the form of frightening nightmares, or continually allude to evil-rooted sexual acts and/or ungodly violence, and you are rooted in your Christian walk, have a good prayer life, are trying to walk in holiness, and still this continues to occur, you may want to consider a discussion or counseling session with a minister who is knowledgeable in is deliverance ministry. But let us not forget that the Lord is not naive and will use many very unusual expressions and revelations that we are familiar with in order to provide us with the protection, correction, and direction we need.

KEYS TO UNLOCKING YOUR DESTINY

- Sexual dreams can be from the Lord. You should not discount them because of sexuality.
- Sex is good in the context of marriage. It illustrates a deep level of commitment and covenant.
- Different forms of sexual activity mean different things to different people.
- If all your revelation is negative in nature or sexual in nature and you are trying to live godly in Christ, you may want to consider counseling, deliverance, or inner healing ministry.

---

[1] *End-Time Warriors*, by John Kelly and Paul Costa (Ventura, California: Regal Books, 1999), p 76.

VESSELS AND FACTORING THEM IN

But we have this treasure in earthen vessels, that the
excellency of the power may be of God, and not of us.
2 CORINTHIANS 4:7

In this chapter, I want to hone in on some specifics concerning interpretation and bring to light factors that can affect and alter the interpretation. As I was contemplating going deeper and further in the understanding, the Lord gave me a dream. In the dream He was plucking and trimming my eyebrows, which told me that He wanted me to do some refining. In this chapter, I want to deal with people, places, things, nature, natural things, direction, and correction, along with timing, in a wide array of vessels.

When dealing with interpretation, vessels are important and meaningful. In the verse this chapter opens with, 2 Corinthians 4:7, an earthen vessel is something that contains the presence of God. As I mentioned previously, vessels can include people, places, things, and vehicles in the overall context of interpretation. Vessels can be good or evil, depending on their use and context in the dream. In any case, the vessel would be symbolic of a person, life, ministry, or mission. I am going to share with you some practical interpretations and illustrations, but first let me refer to 2 Timothy 2:20, which says, *"But in a great house there are not only vessels of gold and of silver, but also of wood and of earth; and some to honour, and some to dishonour."* From this section of scripture, we see that a vessel can be good or evil.

Let me give you some practical examples of vessels. Let's take a boat, which is a vessel: It could mean "your life, your ministry, yourself, or your church"; especially if in the dream it was yours. If in the dream the boat belonged to someone else, then part of the meaning or interpretation would be what that person means to you or how they are related to you. You also need to consider what they do for a living and their ministry function or focus. Who the boat belongs to will give you an identity factor with respect to that person. Consider not only ownership, but use or position in the boat. Were you the pilot? Were you the passenger? Were you one of the group? Who were the others in the group? Obviously, if there are any names or numbers on the boat or vehicle, that would also help you to interpret the dream. Pay attention to the type of boat in your dream: A speedboat would be a fast work. A rowboat represents striving and manual power; powered by man rather than by the Spirit. A party boat, a cruise liner or a battleship would also be a factor in the interpretation.

Let's take into consideration an automobile such as a race car or a pleasure car. A Mercedes or Volkswagen could tell you the size or value. If you dream about trucks, a pickup would be a work vehicle. A meat truck would possibly be teaching for the mature. A milk truck would be foundational teaching for babes in the Lord. A tractor-trailer would be pulling a heavy load or a heavy burden, signifying a lot of responsibility. A tractor-trailer without the trailer would indicate getting free of that load or unencumbered power.

Places are vessels as well. A house or residential living unit is a life or ministry. An apartment building would be a church or ministry with multiple ministries involved. Restaurants many times indicate teaching ministries or places where people are fed. A farm would be a place of harvest. A barn would be a place to store the harvest, or a church that preserves the harvest, or your local church, which is your storehouse. A bar or tavern would be a place where people are under the influence of spirits, which can be either good or evil. The bartender could be the Lord or Satan. A bank would be a church or ministry with power or authority, finances or influence.

Things can be vessels, like a cup, a glass, or a container of sorts. A rock would be the Lord or a solid person in the Lord. A tree is an individual, like "a tree planted by the water". This to me would be a person who is being planted in a good place, a place of revival and refreshing, a place where they are receiving everything they need to grow. A group of people sitting and relaxing in the shade of an old oak tree would be people who were positioned or placed in a church where there was solid teaching and a strong heritage and safe covering. A group of people working in the harvest field would be a church or ministry having to do with evangelism or outreach, or a church that is in the process of bringing in the harvest.

If the building, place, or vessel is in a specific location or scene, that may also help me to interpret or give me direction or correction. For example, if the car is making a u-turn, making a detour, at a stoplight, or coming to a highway and yielding the right-of-way, these would give me specific instructions: possibly to turn around or alter my course. Numbers, times, and colours in your dream are also interpreting factors, as are things of nature like the North Star, the northern lights, the morning light, and sunrise or sunset. One of the most important things is that, as soon as reasonably possibly after receiving the revelation, you record it in writing or on tape and meditate on it. Asking the Lord to prompt your memory with any other details will help you in the interpretation. All of these factors will help you in fine-tuning your interpretation and giving you more specific guidance and direction.

Let's close this chapter with a prayer that the Lord would

impart into the depth of your spirit, the gift of interpretation, and wisdom to bring all the necessary factors together as He stirs your heart with fresh revelation and understanding, by the power and the love of His Spirit. In Jesus' name. Amen.

KEYS TO UNLOCKING YOUR DESTINY

- In the interpretation of dreams, the uses of vessels are both important and meaningful.
- An earthen vessel is something that contains the glory of God.
- Vessels are not limited to just people, but can also signify:
  - Places.
  - Vehicles.
  - Natural things.
- Vessels can be both good and evil depending on their use.

PART 3

PERSONAL DREAMS

PERSONAL DREAMS: PRACTICAL EXAMPLES

This is a very exciting chapter for me. From the very inception of my Christian walk in 1976, God has blessed me with a life led by the Spirit in dreams, visions, and revelation knowledge. From that very first moment, a new spiritual realm became open to me, an awareness of which I had never had before.

Approximately a month and half or maybe fifty days after I was dramatically saved on my kitchen floor, I was baptized in the Holy Ghost, sovereignly. As I was driving down the highway, the presence of God was so strong that I began to weep uncontrollably. I had to pull my car to the side of the road. I got out and lay on my face on the stones in my suit and tie and I began to hear myself speaking in a strange language, and then burst into hearing: "He is the King of kings, the Lord of lords. He is the Beginning and the End, the First and the Last, the Alpha and the Omega. He is the Root and Offspring of David, the Bright Morning Star." The Holy Spirit was giving me the interpretation of the tongues that I was speaking as He baptized me with fire and power. From that moment on, I began to receive the most dramatic visions and dreams nearly every time I went to prayer or to sleep, or even randomly while awake. Over the course of the next six months, these revelations were very intense in nature. He spoke to me and told me to go into business for myself, go into ministry, feed the hungry, and house the homeless. Even in times of Bible study, I would get caught up in revelations. In my spirit, I literally saw Him preaching to the multitudes on the hillside and ministering from a boat just offshore as His followers stood attentively. Many other of the Bible stories literally came alive to me in revelation knowledge. Since I was unchurched, I didn't know anybody who was saved, born again, or filled with the Spirit. I thought all Christians were experiencing this revelation, and I said myself, "This is so exciting. Why didn't they tell me sooner? This is really cool!"

I didn't have relationships with other Christians, so I didn't have access to all the naysayers and wet blankets who, at times, fill our churches and our heads full of doubt and unbelief, and statements that this was for the days of old, or first century Christianity. Consequently, I began my Christian journey unencumbered by religion and entered that exciting life of being led by the Spirit. He used revelation knowledge to birth me into business with no money, experience, or education. At one point, through revelation, He gave me five companies with over two hundred employees and birthed a weekly regional television program that I produced and hosted. Along with that, I couldn't even count all the marketing plans, commercials, meeting agendas, property purchases, divine appointments, and encounters of every type. What a wonderful God we serve: a living, loving, interrelational, and personal God, an intimate God, a God who cares about the little and the large alike. He wants to be a part of your life, if you will let Him. Only believe. Didn't He say, "Only believe"?

Then again, with every revelation comes responsibility. Don't just believe; believe and obey, because He said in His Word that obedience is better than sacrifice. To the Jews who believed in Him, He said, "If you love Me, you will obey Me."

In nearly every large, or important, moment of decision or direction in my life, He gave me revelation and interpretation: a dream, a vision, a prophetic word, or an illumination in the Word, something *rhema* to guide my steps and give me confidence. I'd like to share with you some of those eventful revelations and their practical and personal interpretations, to demonstrate for you and to help you with your walk in the Spirit.

As I mentioned before, as I first began my Christian walk, I had no understanding of church or religion, so the Lord gave me revelation from secular experiences. He put me in business with a series of revelations. First, I would listen to the Steve Miller Band, a rock group at that time. Their cover song, "Fly Like an Eagle," talked about soaring. I was soaring in the Spirit feeding the hungry, housing the homeless, and putting shoes on children who had no shoes. Another song spoke about being carried away on a jetliner, which He used many years later to reveal a large traveling ministry. And later, in the "Fly Like an Eagle" song, which had the lyrics, "Fly like an eagle, to the sea," He brought back to me that revelation as He launched me into ministry in Pensacola, Florida, at the Brownsville Revival School of Ministry, Pensacola being a resort city by the sea.

He showed me in dreams and visions, teaching a small group of people in business seminars, motivating sales people, and teaching trainees. He told me that He was going to put me in business and put a lot of money in my hands and that He wanted me to use it; not just to bless myself and my family, but to bless others who were in need.

I didn't know what field, product, area, or type of business I would be involved in until He moved on me to leave my present position. Right at that pivotal point, my wife and I were watching a newscast on which Vernon Odom was reporting about how the increase in crimes, particularly break-ins and burglaries was causing fear and insecurity in the suburban Philadelphia area. At that time, residential security was not a popular field. However, as he ended his report, he said that in the 1980's there would be either a hundred or hundreds of millionaires in security-related fields. Instantly, my spirit leaped and confirmed what he had said. I turned to my wife and said, "I don't know the other ninety-nine, but I know one of them is me. That's what God wants me to do." I had no idea or previous knowledge of the field, but I knew in my heart that this was it.

As He prompted my spirit, the next day I prepared myself to give notice at my sales job with the insurance company that I worked for. At the time, I was also coaching high school football at Archbishop Kennedy, the local Catholic high school in Conshohocken, Pennsylvania. The following Sunday, I was reviewing the scouting films with my coaching staff, preparing the scouting reports for the next game, and when I returned home, it was rather late. I discovered that my door was unlocked for some reason. When I walked inside, I had an immediate sense of unease. I cried out to my wife and two small children. When we came back downstairs, I knew we had been burglarized. There was a bedsheet laid out on the dining room floor with many of our valuables in it. I had startled the thieves, and they had left it. When I went out back, I noticed that they had stolen my car, which was later found abandoned in a field not too far away. I contacted the police, who conducted a thorough investigation. They found that it was some local teens but were not able to compile enough evidence to prosecute them. My family was safe, my car was recovered, and I had suffered no tangible loss but I had lost my peace of mind. It was a prophetic confirmation of the direction the Lord had given me. This personal experience prepared me to have empathy for burglary victims and helped me to have strong convictions to close literally thousands of sales for residential security systems.

ORDINATION

When I was seeking ordination, the Lord gave me great revelation. I was in my last semester at the Brownsville Revival School of Ministry in Florida and I was seeking the Lord for where He wanted me to be ordained and who He wanted me to be covered by. Knowing I had a prophetic call and had already experienced some signs and wonders in my short time in ministry, I felt it had to be someone special from the Lord for me. I was also working as a testimony worker at Benny Hinn crusades. Two members of his church and crusade team, Paul and Linda McGrath, would regularly call me and we would intercede before the next event, crusade, or conference. After we were through praying, I asked Paul about his ordination. His wife was on the other phone, and she is very prophetic. She said to me, "Brother Russ, the Lord just told me that you are seeking ordination." I told her that I was. She asked me if I knew of Ruth Heflin. I told her that I knew who she was and that I knew her nephew, who was in Bible school with me. She said that Ruth Heflin was going to ordain me. As is my practice when I receive a prophetic word, I prayed into it. That night, the Lord gave me a dream, and in the dream I was running to catch a train and realized that I had forgotten my Bible and would have to run back home and get it. On my way, I passed my home church, Courts of Praise Fellowship, and saw a lady on my intercessory prayer team, Becky Garza. I said to her, "Becky, I don't want to miss my train and I've forgotten my Bible." She handed me her Bible and I ran back to the train station. Just as I got there, the train arrived. The doors opened and I got on. I was out of breath and I was holding the standing strap. After a moment, I realized that I had a women's cover on my Bible, and I said to myself, "I wonder what people will think. I have a woman's cover on my Bible." It was pink with a red rose on it. I then said to myself, "Who cares what they think!" As soon as I said that, the train stopped.

The doors opened and I stepped out onto the platform, and there was Sister Ruth Heflin. She looked like she was ten feet tall and I felt like a midget. She looked down on me and smiled and put her hand on my head and I instantly grew up under her hand. We smiled at each other. She took my arm in her arm and we began to dance on the platform, and then I woke up.

Interpretation – Catching a train has to do with revival ministry. Going to the station is a place of revival, from one place of revival to another (station to station). I was running late; there was a chance I could miss my opportunity—there was an urgency in the revelation. My Bible had to do with my call to preach. Becky was representative of Linda McGrath, the intercessor who had given me the revelation. The cover on my Bible was a woman's cover, meaning that God wanted a woman to cover my ministry. Sister Ruth looked so big and I looked so small–the Lord was showing me the difference in the authority of our two anointings in the prophetic. When I said, "What are the people going to think about a woman's cover on my Bible?" I knew that there were certain people around me who would question whether I could have a woman for a spiritual covering (which, later, they did). My response was very important, "Who cares what they think!" God was trying to tell me how He wanted me to respond and feel. Stepping onto the platform was stepping into a new ministry. When she put her hands on me, it meant the laying of her hands on me for ordination and that I would have rapid spiritual growth. Dancing on the platform meant prophesying or worshiping together. Her revelation was worship; her calling was in the prophetic. The red rose on my Bible was a passion for the glory, and she was the author of the best-selling series on the glory of the Lord.

NEW MANTLE

When I did arrive at Ashland, Sister Ruth ordained me out of season by the prompting of the Spirit. The Spirit of God spoke to her and she immediately did it. I came back to Pensacola thinking I would travel with my pastor, Paul Wetzel. We had some personal plans for ministry since I had worked with him and he had mentored me for over two years. We were very close, but I couldn't seem to get the experience I had in Ashland, Virginia with Sister Ruth Heflin out of my mind. The following Saturday I had a dream, and in the dream there was a blue blazer (sport jacket) flying around in a small room. I started to reach for it but I couldn't get hold of it. Then I started to jump into the air to try to grab it but I still couldn't quite reach it, so I flapped my arms like an eagle and flew up and got it. This meant to me that God was getting ready to give me a mantle but that the experience would stretch me and in order to get it, I would have to get in the Spirit, as this is what flying symbolizes.

The next morning, I went to pick up two young men to go to church, Michael Montabo and Ryan Sellars, whom I was mentoring in the prophetic. On the way, one of them said, "Brother Russ, I had a dream last night, and I believe it's for you." So I asked him what his dream was about. He said he was at camp in Ashland and walked into an empty room that wasn't very big. He opened the closet door and there was a blue sport jacket wrapped in a cleaner's bag. The Lord said He was saving it for me, but I was going to have to go and get it. When I asked him how he knew it was camp, he told me it was very rustic and that the door jambs weren't very straight. Since I have done some construction, this was something that had caught my attention when I was at camp. The door jambs and light switches weren't very straight and it was very rustic. The Lord spoke it to me, confirmed it to Ryan, and within a week I left to go to camp. When I got there, Sister Ruth knew I was coming back to camp. I spent the last ten months of her life there at Ashland, winter camp and summer camp 2000. This was probably my greatest spiritual experience. I grew in my understanding and gifting and in my calling as a prophet and a missionary with a heart for the nations.

TRAVELING MINISTRY

In the fall of 2000, while I was staying with John and Victoria Irving in Toronto, Canada, the Lord spoke to me twice using a large airplane, a jumbo jet. While driving along Highway 401, I had an open vision of a 747 jumbo jet. It said U.S. Air and had a Canadian flag on the tail section. It was suspended in midair right above a bridge on the highway. I thought that I had never seen a plane suspended like that. I soon passed the bridge. When I got home to the Irvings', I asked them if there had been a plane crash and they responded that they had not heard of one. I then told Victoria my vision and she told me that she had seen the same plane in a dream the previous night.

Interpretation – The jumbo jet represents a large traveling ministry. The fact that it was suspended over the bridge represents waiting in a place of faith (a faith ministry). I am a U.S. citizen, which explains U.S. Air, and the Canadian flag represents my call to ministry in Canada. The number 747 represents a fullness and maturity of a place of rest, Kingdom rule and reign, and a complete work.

I had a dream a week later that this same plane had landed in a school yard and there wasn't enough runway for it to get back out. Television crews and newspaper reporters came and interviewed the pilot. He didn't really want to land there and he couldn't get out. All the children and people were excited.

Interpretation – Again, the jumbo jet represents a large traveling ministry. At first, I was afraid and actually put up resistance to the Lord about coming to Canada. My primary call was to the church and to teach and bring the Good News. God was going to make a public announcement. He certainly has been faithful, as we have been well received in nearly sixty churches as well as having planted six of our own. We have also taught School of the Spirit in many locations as well as

School of the Prophets at our summer camp in Copetown, Ontario.

John Irving saw this plane dropping leaflets over the city of Toronto, making announcements about the upcoming services. The Lord also spoke to him in dreams and visions concerning the nature of Eagle Worldwide Ministries. He and his wife, Victoria, hosted me the first seven weeks I was in Canada. They were the only Canadian people I knew prior to my arrival in Canada. I had met them in Ashland, Virginia, at the Calvary Pentecostal Campground of the Heflin family. The Lord called them to pastor The Gathering Place which is the first church I planted in Aurora, Ontario. Pastor John Irving is also the vice-president of Eagle Worldwide Ministries.

REVIVAL MINISTRY

In one of his dreams, John Irving saw me on a one-humped camel. I was beginning a journey across the desert, from east to west. It was a large desert, like North Africa. Many people tried to stop me, saying it was too hard and that I wouldn't succeed. Difficult times would lie ahead if I proceeded. Yet in his dream, I went ahead. After I had traveled for a while, two or three others on camels joined me and I continued to lead out in front. A while later, more people on camels joined in and we traveled westward across the desert. About halfway across, a multitude of people on camels joined the group and covered the entire desert behind us. I led them into a place of refreshing, and the desert began to bloom and life began to come throughout that desert.

Interpretation – The one-humped camel is symbolic of the vehicle or ministry that is best suited for a dry ground, for a desert journey could go on for a long time without water/refreshing. He said we were beginning the journey; this was at the inception of Eagle Worldwide Ministries. East has to do with new beginnings, as in the dawning of a new day. West has to do with the end, the setting sun, start to finish, grace, and conformity. The natural interpretation is that we were in the south-eastern portion of Ontario. Since then, our ministry has progressed westward, towards Alberta and British Columbia. and even the western portions of Ontario. The large desert— Canada is a large country. The desert is probably symbolic of the overall spiritual climate of the church in Canada at that time. North Africa would be North America, as Canada is situated in North America. The initial "A" for Africa can represent "A" for America. The people trying to stop me means that there was going to be spiritual opposition and hindrance to revival in Canada. "It's hard and you won't succeed," and many people at that time were telling me the same thing: that Canada was a hard place and I wouldn't succeed; that others had tried without success. I never confirmed what they said or spoke it over myself or the nation because I know that there is nothing impossible for God. Then the dream said that we continued to go ahead. He was telling us to persist and go on despite what people were saying. Traveling for a while would mean making progress, walking means progress. After a while two or three others on camels joined us. Two or three is to discern, conform, and obey in a positive sense and meant that I was to continue to lead. As I was out in front, this means that the revelation was for the future. Going west here means grace. Then more people were going to join us—a multitude, until they filled the entire desert behind me. The multitude of people symbolizes a large company. Leading them to a place of refreshing means coming to a place of revival. The desert blooming means coming back to life throughout the desert. I believe this means revival throughout Canada. The latter portion of the revelation, with the people joining and following after me, and others saying that it would be hard and trying to discourage me, was a confirmation of the prophetic word that Ruth Heflin spoke over my life on January 7, 2000, when she ordained me into ministry. Here is an excerpt from that prophetic word.

> *Not by might, nor by power, but by My Spirit, saith the Lord. Not by might, nor by power, but by My Spirit, saith the Lord—and Heaven's help shall be laid upon thee, great help, great help from the heavenlies. Great help shall be laid upon thee, and you shall have wings that will cause thee to soar again and again. You shall soar from the earthly and you shall soar into the heavenly, and I shall give you the ability to cause others to soar with thee. I shall use thee to create hunger in their hearts for more. Those who have become self-satisfied and complacent shall suddenly long for more, for I shall cause them to hear the glory in your voice, and see the glory on your face, and feel the glory in your touch, and when they experience the glory they shall run after it, they shall run after Me, saith the Lord. And I will cause a company to follow after thee, for some have said none would follow thee, but they shall, they shall, they shall. There shall be a great company that shall rise up and follow after thee and thou shalt look behind thee and feel the sense of great responsibility as many come from here and there and everywhere. From here and there and everywhere, here and there and everywhere shall they come, and they shall follow after thee, as you follow after Me, saith the Lord.*

This dream given to pastor John Irving is a confirmation of that prophetic word spoken over me by Sister Ruth Heflin on January 7, 2000.

In another dream, John Irving saw a place that was said to be impossible to build a road through. There was a rock formation that people did not want to destroy because of its unusual shape; however, it blocked a connection with two roads. It was on the coast—by the Atlantic Ocean in Labrador, east of Quebec. There was also a small island that could not be reached because of the rock formation. This was a two-fold problem—no connection for the roads or to the island—said to be impossible to solve by the locals and the experts. Someone had a dream to find a solution. He worked hard but had many failures. Finally, he came up with a most unusual design. The center of the rock formation was made into a large moveable object that actually came out and became a helicopter to reach the island, and when it came out, it created a hole in the center that connected both roads but did not hurt the natural attraction of this rock formation. Newspaper and TV reporters flocked to report this wonder. People were amazed that the impossible had been accomplished. Pastor John recalled that one local person was not happy because it affected his ferry boat business to the island.

Interpretation – The rock formation was so large and unusual that many people came to see it because it was a sign and wonder. This probably signifies the work the Lord is doing being rock solid, being large, a work of signs and wonders. In the dream, many people had a negative outlook saying that it was impossible, which was typical of what was being said when I came to Canada in 2000. We believe that the whole dream had to do with revival in Canada, and to build a road through would be symbolic of a long road, a path to follow or a blueprint—an unusual work. Labrador, Quebec, and the Atlantic Ocean, all point to the subject being Canada; east being as sunrise—something starting, dawning, or beginning. Some opposition on a local basis, some hard-to-reach places, islands, or areas are ministries that may have a trouble connecting or accepting the work. The center would be the heart of the traveling ministry, because when it came out of the rock, it was a helicopter, symbolic of short-term ministry trips. When the helicopter was out to where the ministry team was going, there would still remain a flow of traffic, or anointing, at the crossroads. We are located in an area that's called "Copetown—the Hub of the Universe," and we are also close to a television and radio ministry known as Crossroads here in Ontario, Canada. The local person who was not happy because it affected his ferry business to the island is symbolic of the opposition that we have experienced from some folks in ministry with a local focus, rather than a Kingdom vision.

Network of Ministries

Before I started Eagle Worldwide Network of Ministries, the Lord gave me a dream that I was standing in front of a large high-rise building with many windows. The top floors were residential units (apartments/condos). There was a helicopter pad on the roof. The lower floors were offices—commercial businesses. I was standing out front looking at it with a friend who I knew. My friend was a woman, but I didn't recognize her. We both had yellow hard hats on. There were window washers all over the building. I said to my friend, "I know I'm not the owner and only the manager, but I have to treat it like it was my own. I will subcontract a lot of the work." It was a very sunny day.

Interpretation – Standing out front means a future revelation. The sunshine from the sunny day is the Lord shining the light and revelation. Multiple units speak of many ministries connected together with me. Many windows represent a ministry of revelation and prophecy. The window cleaners will help me to see more clearly in the Spirit. The helicopter pad means that many will come and go—traveling ministries. The apartments are temporary ministries, while the condos represent those permanent to the work. Part of the ministry will be dedicated to marketplace ministry, as defined by the commercial business units. The yellow hard hats represent covering and spiritual gifts. The woman friend is an angel of the Lord, my wife, Mave, or Pastor Carol from Jehovah Jireh, who also sits on the Network board. I know that this work will not be mine, but I will manage the work.

As I mentioned before, in almost every situation and on almost a daily basis, the Lord led my life by dreams and visions. This has been the key in making major decisions and directional moves, along with covenant relationships.

Just a couple more quick examples, but I could fill the whole book. In fact, I have filled many books. I bring a dream book with me every night and record all that I see and hear: dates, times, and other details. I try to keep a well-organized file of those revelations with the help of several people in our ministry. I also keep a file on revelation that comes from my intercessors and people in key relationship with me who walk in godly ways. Many times, I'll refer back to those revelations for confirmation, encouragement, and edification: all the things that the prophetic gift was meant to provide individually and collectively in the body.

My Marriage to Mave

When I was working my way through the process of deciding to marry my wife, Mave, the Lord gave me a number of dreams and revelations along with many promptings and confirmations. As many women may know, many of my gender can have a tendency to be a little slow getting the message on marriage. In one dream, there were two high-back matching chairs in front of a large picture window. I was sitting next to a woman who was going back and forth between myself and my niece, Christina. For many years, I was in covenant with Christina, who was my administrative assistant. This was Mave's position at the time. We were looking out the front picture window.

Interpretation – Looking out the window is future revelation.

The high-back chairs represent authority. Sitting side by side means unity. Joan Gieson was in the dream. She was exhorting me and telling me all these good things about Mave. I rebuked her, saying that it was not right to prophesy marriage and pray. In real life, Joan, who worked eight years with Kathryn Kuhlman and eight years with Benny Hinn, introduced Mave and me. We both worked with and have an ongoing relationship with Joan. She had prophesied to Mave about our relationship. Obviously, from my response in the dream, I had not yet stepped into a receptive mode.

In another revelation, I was on Fourth Street in my hometown. A big parade was going on. My high school principal was in the parade. I was standing next to my ex-wife. When he saw me, he came over and told me about his daughter who had been to Bible school, and was a good teacher and preacher and knew the Word. He kept going on and on. I said to him, "What about me?" I'd gone to Bible school too and knew the Word. Then he went on about his business. I walked my ex-wife home, knowing it wasn't meant to be for her and me because she had closed the door behind her. I turned and saw a Chip Wagon across the street. There were stools attached to the front, and a woman with a large white cowboy hat was seated there. In the mirror above the grill, I could see the woman's face. It was Mave. I thought she saw me and wondered what she thought about my conversation. I walked over and saw a cook, grilling. Mave said, "Sit down; the food's good." I asked her what was cooking and she said, "Possum stew." When we were through, the cook said that Mave was a "good egg."

Interpretation – The parade signifies a big happening or event. At the time, I was still standing in old thoughts concerning my previous life and family. The principal was the Lord, telling me about Mave (His daughter) and bragging on her gifts and callings. I was self-centered and seeing only myself. Taking a walk means making progress. The fact that my ex-wife had closed the door means an end to an old relationship. Mave with a cowboy hat and sitting at the grill speaks of her background as a country singer and being a restaurant owner. Sitting next to her to eat means coming into relationship. Possum stew is one of her comedy lines and is symbolic of a sleeper. As Mave stepped into various roles in the ministry, her gifts and callings were revealed. Something cooking is something happening. Her being across the street means a current revelation. A good egg represents a vehicle of birthing (an egg brings life), and also means a promise in the prophetic.

Again, in interpretation, all of these emotions, times, colours, dates and symbols are important and can be relevant and different depending on our personal life history, understanding, and background. The Lord speaks personally to all of us as well as biblically and in simple logic. He also speaks in allegories, parables, riddles, or symbols. There are many factors in the interpretation process and many variables that all personalize, and can have an effect on, the interpretation and direction we receive.

THE TITLE AND COVER FOR THIS BOOK

When we had the book finished Mave and I prayed for the Lord to title it and give us a cover. Mave had a dream early in the morning of the northern lights. Everywhere she looked she saw beautiful pastel colours, and the North Star. When she awoke and shared her dream, I said to her that the North Star is used for direction. We drifted back to sleep and the book stood right up before her with the northern lights and the title "Night Watch" We knew that this was God's choice. He had shown her exactly how it would look, even the way we were to make the letters on Night Watch. Truly in the night, we are called to stand watch in the Spirit and see what the Lord might say to us. Serving Him is an ever changing, always exciting way of life. Abundant life!!! Thank you Lord, for speaking to your people, and causing us to succeed.

Keys to Unlocking Your Destiny

- God can use secular revelation and information to convey His message.
- Be careful not to share your revelation with those who may not have an understanding of how you are trying to live.
- God wants to be involved in all aspects of our lives, in the large things and in the small things.
- He will use others to bring confirmation. Some may be prophets or friends who are Christian, and some may be unbelievers in secular settings and careers.
- God brings confirmation to increase our faith and confidence, to help us dare to take bold steps into uncharted waters.

PART 4

DREAM SYMBOLS

DREAM SYMBOLS

*Now as I beheld the living creatures, behold one wheel
upon the earth by the living creatures, with his four faces.
The appearance of the wheels and their work was like unto
the colour of a beryl: and they four had one likeness: and
their appearance and their work was as it were a wheel in
the middle of a wheel.*

EZEKIEL 1:15-16

The Lord spoke to Ezekiel, Daniel, John the Revelator, and King Nebuchadnezzar, along with many other biblical characters, in symbols. It's important to realize that when He speaks to you or me symbolically, in addition to the general or natural interpretation of the symbols, characters, numbers, colours, circumstances, or things, there is also a personal, or individual interpretation. The Lord speaks to us individually because He knows the sum total of our personal experiences and the inventory of our knowledge. If He speaks to me concerning football, golf, or other sports, it has a greater depth of meaning for me, because of my life experience as an athlete and coach, than it would for a layman/spectator or someone who has never had any experiences in athletics. By the same token, He speaks to my wife, who has had a lot of experience in the restaurant, theater, and entertainment industry, with depth in particulars that have completely different meaning for her than for me. Our God is a personal God, and one of the most wonderful things about hearing from Him in dreams, visions, and symbols, is that many times, they confirm the fact that He knows me. He really knows me. And there is nothing more comforting than knowing that God really knows you.

Interpretation is by no means an exact science. I can give you input, but in the end, it's between you and the Lord what He is saying to you, what He means, and what He wants you to do with it. The following symbols are an inventory of the vocabulary He has used to speak with me over the years; there are many more, of course, but these may help you. Some have a natural or biblical base; some are based on information I have received from others or from my own personal study. Because of the nature of my calling, I find it enjoyable to read and study prophetic people and to see and analyze how God speaks to them. Most of these symbols, you will find have multiple meanings that you can alter to meet the circumstance or mood or climate of the revelation, be it good, evil, threatening, or exhilarating. I will believe the Lord with you, that He will expand your vocabulary with Him and grant you revelation, understanding, and wisdom. In Jesus' name, Amen.

NUMBERS

ONE—Beginning: First—in time, rank, order, or importance; new.
(Genesis1:5b) (Genesis 8:13)

TWO—Divide: Judge; separate; discern; subdivide.
(Genesis 1:6, 8b) (1 Kings 3:25, 28)

THREE—Conform: Obey; copy; imitate; likeness; tradition; the Trinity. (Genesis 1:9, 11, 13) (Romans 8:29)

FOUR—Reign: Rule (over the world); Kingdom; creation (including things in Heaven and earth); world.
(Genesis 1:16, 18-19)

FIVE—Serve: Works; service; bondage (including debt, sickness, phobias, etc.); taxes; prison; sin; motion.
(Genesis 1:20, 23) (Genesis 41:34) (Leviticus 27:31) (John 8:34)

SIX—Image: Man; flesh; carnal; idol; form.
(Genesis 1:26a, 31b) (Revelation 13:18)

SEVEN—Complete: All; finished; rest.
(Genesis 2:1, 3)

EIGHT—Put Off (as in putting off "the old man," i.e., the works of the flesh): Sanctify; manifest; reveal; die; death. By implication, new beginning (the result of putting off the old life is a new life or beginning).
(Genesis 17:12) (2 Chronicles 29:17) (1 Peter 3:20-21) (2 Peter 1:14)

NINE—Harvest: Fruit; fruitfulness; fruition.
(Luke 17:17) (Romans 6:22) (Judges 4:1-3)

TEN—Measure (for the purpose of accepting or rejecting that which is measured): Try or trial; test or to be tested; temptation. (Daniel 5:27) (Matthew 18:21-22; see also Matthew 18:23-35)

NOTE: The meanings of the numbers 11 through 19 are antonyms of the numbers 1 through 9. (In other words, they are the reverse of the result of the application of the base numbers, 1 through 9.) For example, 3 means to *"conform"*. The opposite of conforming and the result of forced conformity is rebellion. Therefore 13 means to *rebel*. (See THREE and THIRTEEN)

When a base number is multiplied by 10, to obtain the meaning, couple the key word of the base number with the thought of acceptance or rejection. For example, the date 5/5/50 means "service accepted" (or "rejected," as the case may be); 5 means "to *serve*", 10 means "to measure for the purpose of accepting or rejecting" — therefore 5 times 10 equals "service accepted/rejected." (See TWENTY)

ELEVEN—End: Finish; last; stop.
(Matthew 20:9, 12)

TWELVE—Joined: United; govern; government; oversight. (Government is the means by which people are united into common purposes and goals.)
(Luke 9:1-2) (Luke 22:30) (1 Corinthians 1:10)

THIRTEEN—Rebel: Rebellion; revolution; rejection.
(Genesis 14:4)

FOURTEEN—Double: Re-create; reproduce; disciple; servant; bond slave (employee).
(1 Kings 8:65)

FIFTEEN—Free: Grace; liberty; sin covered; honour.
(2 Kings 20:6a) (Hosea 3:2a) (Genesis 7:20)

SIXTEEN—Spirit: Free-spirited; without boundaries; without limitation; without law (and therefore without sin); salvation. (Acts 27:34, 37-38)

SEVENTEEN—Incomplete: Immature; undeveloped; unfinished; childish; naive; a babe in Christ. (Genesis 37:2) (Jeremiah 32:9, 15)

EIGHTEEN—Put On: Judgment; destruction; captivity; overcome; put on (the Spirit of) Christ. (Judges 10:7-8) (Luke 13:4) (Luke 13:11,16)

NINETEEN—Barren: Ashamed; repentant; selflessness; without self-righteousness. (2 Samuel 2:30) (Romans 6:21)

TWENTY—Holy: Tried and approved (or unholy: tried and found wanting). Two = *Separated*. Ten = *Measured*. (See TWO and TEN) (Revelation 4:4)

FORTY—Testing: Trial; temptation. (Matthew 4:2)

FIFTY—Pentecost: Liberty; freedom; jubilee. (Leviticus 23:16) (Acts 2:1)

SEVENTY-FIVE—The number of Separation: Cleansing; purifying. (Genesis 12:4)

HUNDRED—Fullness: Full measure; full recompense; full reward; etc. (Genesis 26:12) (Mark 10:30)

THOUSAND—Maturity: Full stature; mature service; mature judgment; etc. (Joshua 3:3-4) (1 Samuel 17:5, 33) (Ephesians 4:13)

SYMBOLS

ADULTERY—Sin: Idolatry; pornography. Evil covenant; breaking or violating covenant relationship.

AIRPLANE—Life, Travel, or Traveling Ministry: Team ministry. Small airplane = *Personal ministry.* Flying or soaring = *Moved by the Spirit;* ministering in the gifts of the Spirit. Flying too low = *Insufficient power (prayer) or preparation (training).* Airplane Crash = *Failure;* church or ministry split; personal disaster (a failed marriage, business venture, etc.). Fighter Jet = *Warfare ministry.*

AIRPORT—Base or Port for Traveling Ministry or a Large Church: A base for multiple traveling ministries that come in and out of the base. Natural interpretation or personal travel.

ALLIGATOR (OR CROCODILE)—Ancient: Evil out of the past; Leviathan; danger; destruction; evil spirit. (See BEAR)

AMBER—The Glory of God: Caution; yield.

ANCHOR—Hold Steady: Keep in place; a heavy load.

ANKLES—Faith, Support: Weak ankles = *Weak faith; unsupported; undependable.*

ANT—Industrious: Wise; diligent; nuisance.

ANTIQUES—Past: Inherited from our forefathers (good or evil). Inheritance; memories.

APPLES—Fruit: Words; temptation; appreciation (as in "an apple for the teacher"); fruit of the Spirit.

ARM—Strength or Weakness: Saviour; deliverer; helper; aid; reaching out.

ARRESTED—Stopped: Illegal; unauthorized; penalty; wrong; judgment.

ARROWS—See BOW/ARROWS

ASHES—Memories (that which has been reduced to ashes remains only in memory): Repentance; ruin; destruction.

ATTIC—Mind: Thought; attitude; memories stored.

AUTOMOBILE—Life: Person; ministry. New car = *New ministry or new way of life.* Automobile breakdown = *Problem; sickness; trouble; opposition; hindrance.* Limousine = *Important; pride.*

> CONVERTIBLE (with the Top up)—Covered: Protected covering or covenant.

> CONVERTIBLE (with the Top down)—Uncovered: Everything revealed; open, nothing hidden; a self-righteous or unsaved person; "living in the fast lane."

AUTO WRECK OR CRASH—Strife; defeat; failure: Contention; conflict; confrontation; mistake or sin in ministry.

AUTUMN—End: Completion; change; repentance.

BABY—New: Beginning; new idea; new work (church); dependent; helpless; innocent; sin; natural baby.

BACK (BACKYARD OR BACKDOOR)—Past: Previous event or experience (good or evil); that which is behind (in time: for example, your past sins or the sins of your forefathers).

BACKWARD (as in DIRECTION)—Retreat: Reverse; demote; into your past; regress; backslide.

BAKER—Instigator: One who cooks up (and serves) ideas; originator; Christ; Satan; minister; self.

BANK—Secure: Dependable; safe; reward reserved in heaven; the Church. A place of power; storehouse.

BARBERSHOP—Church: A place of removal of old covenants of sin, occult, or religion.

BARN—Storehouse: Church; relating to the work of the ministry; provision; large work.

BASEBALL GAME—Worship: Play; sports; team ministry. Take note if you are participating or just a spectator.

BASEMENT—Soul: Carnal nature; lust; discouragement or depression; refuge; hidden; forgotten; secret sin; stored.

BAT—Witchcraft: Flighty; unstable. Blind or poor vision.

BATHING—Cleansing: Sanctification; repentance.

BATHROOM—Deliverance or Cleansing: Prayer of repentance; confession of offenses or sins to another person.

BATTERY—Power: Strength; prayer; motivation.

BEAR—Destroyer: Destruction; an evil curse (through inheritance or personal sin, including financial loss or hardship); economic loss; danger; opposition; Russia.

BEARD—Covering: Humanity, relating to the heart. Rough, unshaven face = *Spiritual neglect or uncleanness*; coarse or harsh personality.

BEAUTY SHOP—Church: Preparation; vanity; holiness.

BEAVER—Industrious: Busy; diligent; clever; ingenious; Canada.

BED—Rest: Salvation; meditation; intimacy; peace; covenant or an evil covenant; self-made conditions.

BEDROOM—Rest: Place of intimacy; private place.

BEES—Chastisement or Offense: Stinging words; affliction; busybody; busy; gossip. Honeybees = *cross-pollination*.

BELLS—Sign indicating: (1) Change (as in "the times are changing"). (2) God's presence (as in "church bells"). (3) Marriage (Wedding bells).

BELLY—Spirit: Desire; lust; heart; feelings; selfishness; self-worship; sickness. Centre (as in "the belly of a ship" or the "belly of the whale", or "inside").

BESTIALITY—Inordinate Lust: Unnatural, deviant sexual acts; obscene.

BIBLE—Word: Law; holy; solid; stand; first; final.

BICYCLE—Works: Works of the flesh; working out life's difficulties. Bicycle built for two = *Working together;* a couple in ministry.

BIKINI—Uncovered: Carnal; seduction; temptation; insufficient covering.

BILLS/DEBTS—Curse: Penalty; obligation; responsibility.

BINGO—Winner or Correct: Sudden victory; correct answer, idea.

BINOCULARS—Insight: Understanding; prophetic vision; future event; looking ahead.

BIRD—Spirit: Holy Spirit; demon; man; gossip; message. Dirty or unclean (as in "a dirty bird").

BLACK—Lack: Sin; ignorance; grief; mourning; gloomy; evil; famine; burned.

BLACK TIE—Formal or important. If evil, shows ranking spirits.

BLACK AND WHITE—Either Good or Bad; plain and simple. No gray area.

BLACKJACK—Gambling; high risk; evil game.

BLEEDING—Wounded: Hurt (bodily or emotionally); spiritually dying; gossip; unclean (e.g., the woman with the issue of blood).

BLIND—Ignorance: Unseeing; without understanding; unlearned; foolish; self-justification and self-righteousness.

BLOOD—Life: Covenant; murder; defiled; unclean; pollution; purging; testimony; witness; guilt.

BLOOD TRANSFUSION—Change: Regeneration; new life; salvation.

BLUE—Spiritual: Spiritual gift; divine revelation; heavenly visitation; depressed (as in "singing the blues"); a baby boy.

BOAR—Persecutor: Hostile to virtue; vicious; vengeful; danger; wild; attack.

BOAT—Ministry: Life; person; recreation; spare time. Large ship = *The Church*. Small boat = *Personal ministry*. Sailboat = *Moved by the Spirit*. Powerboat = *Powerful ministry or fast progress*. Battleship = *Spiritual warfare*; rescue. Shipwreck = *Church split*; ministry failure; error or accident. Rowboat = *Striving*; power of self; works.

BODY ODOUR—Uncleanness: Bad attitude; filthiness of the flesh; rejected.

BOMB—Power: Holy Spirit outpouring; miracle power; sudden destruction.

BONES—Spirit: Condition of the heart; death; that which is eternal; structure.

BOOK—Record: Word of God; heart of man; witness; remembrance; conscience; education; knowledge. Book of life. Open book = *Life revealed;* transparent.

BOOTS—Hard Work of ministry: Army boots = *Warfare*. Cowboy boots = *Wild ride;* pioneer work.

BOW/ARROWS—Words: Accusations; slander; attack; gossip; prayer; deliverance. Quiver = *Heart;* safe place; hidden.

BOWL—Vessel: Doctrine; tradition or person.

BOXING—Striving: Preaching; deliverance; trial; tribulation. Contest; competition; fighting; strife.

BRAKES—Stop: Hindrance; resist; wait. Brakes failing = *Not able to discontinue a bad habit or change a tradition;* no resistance to temptation.

BRASS—Word: Word of God; judgment; hypocrisy; self-justification; fake; man's tradition; word of man.

BREAD—Life or Word: Doctrine; covenant; substance; provision.

BRIDE—Church: Covenant; natural marriage when naturally interpreted.

BRIDGE—Support or Way: Faith; trial; joined; connections; intercession; standing in the gap. Unifying (as in "building bridges").

BRIERS—Snare: Obstacle; hindrance; trial; wicked person; rejected; cursed. Uncomfortable place.

BROOM—Cleaning or Witchcraft: Clean house.

BROTHER—Self: Natural or spiritual brother; someone he reminds you of. Close friend; fellow member of church.

BROTHER-IN-LAW—Fellow Minister: Someone he reminds you of; problem relationship; partner; oneself; he may represent himself.

BROWN—Dead (As Dead Grass Is Brown): Repented; born again; without spirit.

BUBBLE GUM—Childish: Foolishness; silliness; immaturity; sticky; rebellion.

BULL—Persecution: Spiritual warfare; opposition; accusation; slander; threat; economic increase.

BULLETS—Words: Accusations; warfare; attack.

BUS—Church: School bus = *Teaching or youth/children's ministry.* Passenger or tour bus = *Trip;* journey. Team ministry; Christians; sight-seers.

BUS STATION—Church: Ministry location.

BUTTER—Works: Doing the Word or will of God. Deceptive motives; words; smooth talker; deceiver.

BUTTERFLY—Freedom: Flight (flitting about); fragile; temporary glory; move. Cocoon = *Metamorphosis;* transformation;

change. New beginnings; something not yet revealed. Caterpillar = *Devourer;* potential; danger or potential good.

BUZZARD—Vulture: Scavenger, something dying.

CAFETERIA—Service: Church; people or work; teaching; ministry of helps.

CALENDAR—Time: Date; event; appointment. Refer to Numbers for symbolic interpretation.

CALF—Increase: Prosperity; idolatry; false worship; stubbornness; children of the Kingdom.

CAMEL—Endurance: Long journey; contention.

CAPITAL—Important: First in order; emphasis; government.

CAR—Ministry: Life. New car = *New life or ministry.* Antique car = *Valuable or old-fashioned.* Race car = *Fast/powerful ministry.*

CARDS—Facts: Honesty (as in "putting all your cards on the table"); truth; expose or reveal; dishonesty; underhanded dealing; cheating; wisdom (as in "knowing when to hold and when to fold").

CARNIVAL—Worldly: Festivity; party spirit; exhibitionism; divination; competition.

CARPENTER—Builder: Preacher; evangelist; labourer; Christ.

CAT—Self-willed: Witchcraft. Not trainable (unteachable spirit); predator; unclean spirit. Sneaky; crafty; deception. Personal pet = *Something precious.*

CHAIR—Rest or Position: Place; quietness; position of authority. Type of chair would define rank or position of authority.

CHECK/CHEQUE—Faith: Provision; trust. Bad check = *Fraud*; deception; hypocrisy; lack of faith or prayer. When amount is known, refer to numbers for symbolic meaning.

CHEESE—Works: Doing (or not doing) the Word or will of God.

CHEWING—Meditate: Receiving wisdom and understanding. Chewing bubble gum = *Childishness;* foolishness. Chewing tough meat = *Hard saying or difficult work.*

CHICKEN—Fear: Unclean; cowardliness. Chick = *Defenseless;* innocent. Baby or babe in the Lord.

CHOCOLATE/CANDY—Treats: Blessings; feel good but without strength; teaching or discipline (candy-coated) that has no nutritional value or substance, but only makes the one who partakes feel good temporarily.

CHOKING—Hindrance: Stumbling over something (as in "hard to swallow"); hatred or anger (as in "I could choke him!"); un-fruitful (as in "the thorns sprang up and choked them").

CHRISTMAS—Gift: Season of rejoicing; spiritual gifts; a surprise; good will; benevolence; commercialism. Spiritual birthing. Visitation of God.

CHURCH BUILDING—Church: Congregation; may represent one's own church or ministry.

CIGARETTES (SMOKING)—Pride: Dangerous; hazardous to your health, rebellion.

CITY—A Church: Natural place; a call. Reference to what a city may be known for or by. Example: Philadelphia = *City of Brotherly Love*. Pensacola = *Revivals*; seaside resort.

CLOCK—Time: Late; early; delay. Grandfather clock = *Past* (see significant and specific numbers for symbolism).

CLOSET—Private: Personal; prayer; secret sin (as in "skeletons in the closet"); something hidden.

CLOTHING—Covering: Righteousness; spirit. Dirty clothes = *Unrighteousness;* self-righteousness; uncleanness.

CLOUDS—Change or Covering: Trouble; distress; threatening; thoughts (of trouble); confusion; hidden; covered. White Clouds = *Good change;* glory; revival; refreshing on the way.

CLOWN—Fool: Foolish works of the flesh; the "old man"; childish; mischief. Crying clown = *laughing on the outside*, crying on the inside.

COAT—Covering: Anointing; authority; protection.

COFFEE—Bitter or Stimulant: Desire for revenge; bitter memories.

COMPASS—Directions: Help to find your way (for specifics, refer to north, south, east, and west); finding your path; Holy Spirit your guide; getting your bearings.

CORD—To Connect: Bound up cord of three strands = *Strong bond*.

CORNUCOPIA (HORN OF PLENTY)—Abundance: Abundance without measure or limitation; goodness without end; blessed.

COUCH—Rest: At ease; unconcerned; lazy.

COUNTRY—Isolated: Quiet; peaceful; restful. Nation: Reference to what that country may be known for or by. Example: U.S.A.= *Freedom.*

COURTHOUSE—Judgment: Trial; persecution; justice; legal matter.

COW—Prosperity (Cash Cow): Wealth. Heifer = *Prize or rebellious woman.*

CRIMSON—Blood Atonement: Sacrifice of death.

CROSSROADS—Decision: Confusion; choice; job change; career change; geographic move.

CROOKED—Twisted: Spiritually distorted; out of alignment; unrighteous; unbiblical; doctrinal error.

CROW/RAVEN—Confusion: Outspoken person, usually operating under the influence of a spirit of envy or strife; God's minister of justice or provision.

CROWN—Authority or Reward: Rule; honour; glory; power; promotion.

CRYING—Sadness: Compassion; grief; repentance; sorrow.

CRYING OUT—Calling for Help: Praying earnestly.

CRYSTAL BALL—Vision: Future; prediction; divination; fortune telling; witchcraft; sorcery.

CURTAIN—Hidden: Divided; separated; hindrance to revelation.

DAM—Reserve: Source of (or potential for) great power; block; restriction; hindrance; a way over an obstacle.

DANCING—Worship: Idolatry; prophesying; joy; romance; seduction; lewdness.

DAUGHTER—Child: Natural or spiritual; wife (see ONE'S CHILDREN)

DAY—Light: Knowledge; truth; manifest; good; evil revealed.

DEAD-END ROAD OR STREET—Change directions: Stop; repent; certain failure; no advancement possible (as in "a dead-end job").

DEATH—Termination: Repentance; loss; sorrow; failure; separation; the end of a relationship; physical death, when naturally interpreted.

DEED—Ownership: Authority; power; rights.

DEER—Graceful: Swift; sure-footed; agile; timid. Buck = *Regal*; rule. Antlers = *Power*; authority.

DEN—Comfortable Place: Family place; safe place. Evil place (den of iniquity) where sin occurs.

DESERT—Barren: Unproductive; dry; spiritual wasteland; without hope.

DESSERT—Finishing Touch: Special treat ("icing on the cake"); topping things off.

DETOUR—Change in Direction: Alter your course; temporary change; new course of action.

DIAMOND—Hard: Unchangeable; hard-hearted; eternal (as in "a diamond is forever"). Gift of the Spirit; something valuable or precious.

DISH—See POT/PAN/BOWL

DITCH—Habit or Snare: Religious tradition; addiction; lust; passion; sin; rut.

DIVORCE—Broken Covenant: Sin; alone; defeat; separate; division; split.

DOCTOR—Healer: Authority; Christ; preacher; medical doctor.

DOG—Strife: Contention; offense; unclean spirit. Personal pet = *Something precious*, or a friend. Dog wagging tail = *Friendly;* acceptance. Tucked tail = *Guilt;* shame; cowardly. Biting Pet = *Rewarding evil for good* (as in "biting the hand that feeds you"); betrayal; unthankful. Barking dog = *Warning;* incessant nuisance; annoyance. Dog trailing game = *Persistent;* obsession. Rabid dog = *Single-minded pursuit of evil;* contagious evil; persecution; great danger.

BULLDOG—Unyielding: Stubborn, obstinate; tenacious; dangerous.

WATCHDOG—Watchman: Elder; minister (good or bad); alert; beware.

DOMINOES—Continuous: Chain reaction.

DONKEY—Obnoxious: Self-willed; stubborn; unyielding; tenacious.

DOOR—Entrance: Christ; enter; authority; go; way; avenue; mouth. Open = *Opportunity*. Closed = *Stop;* seal; safe.

DOVE—Holy Spirit: Gentle; peace.

DOWN—Demotion (Spiritual or Natural): Backslide; falling away; humility; indication of mood; depression.

DRESS—Covering: Protection. Discern the type of dress for further clarification.

DRIVER—Control: Self; Christ; pastor; teacher; Satan; the emphasis may be on the nature of the driver (careless, careful, frantic, confident, selfish, rude, kind, etc.). Passenger = *Self;* church member; family member. When a school bus driver represents a teacher, his passengers usually represent his students.

DROUGHT—Blessing Drying Up: Blessing withheld; wilderness experience; without God's presence.

DROWNING—Overcome: Self-pity; depression; temptation; backslidden; excessive debt. (See FLOOD)

DRUGS—Influence: Spell; sorcery; witchcraft; control; medicine; healing.

DRUNK—Influenced: Under a spell; controlled; addicted; fool; unchangeable; stubborn; rebellious; selfish; self-indulgent; out of control.

DYNAMITE—Power: Miracle; potential; danger; destruction.

EAGLE—Leader: Prophet; powerful; great vision; minister; fierce predator; sorcerer. America. Free; independent.

EARTHQUAKE—Upheaval: Change, thus repentance; trial; God's judgment; disaster; trauma; shock; shaking.

EAST—Beginning: Law of Moses (therefore blessed or cursed); birth; first; anticipate; sun rising; beginning.

EATING—Partake: Participate; experience; outworking; covenant; agreement; friendship; fellowship; devour; consume.

ECHO—Repetition: Gossip; accusation; voice of many; mocking; mimic.

EGG—Promise: Promising new thought; plan; potential; revelation; fragile. Rotten egg = *Bad person* (as in "he's a bad egg"); a person who breaks promises; bad company; bad idea; uncertainty (as in "don't count your eggs [chickens] before they hatch"); without promise.

ELECTRICITY—Power: Holy Spirit or sorcery. Power Lines = *Spiritual power;* dangerous obstacle when flying.

ELEPHANT—Invincible or Thick-skinned: Not easily offended; powerful, large; good memory. Elephant ears = *Extra sensitive hearing*. Baby elephant = *Potential for greatness* (the beginning of something large). White elephant = *Unusable item;* unsalable; unwanted.

ELEVATOR—Changing Position: Going into the spiritual realm; elevated. Going up = *Promotion*. Going down = *Demotion or trial;* backsliding.

EMPLOYEE—Servant: Fellow employee = *Self;* another employee, or the actual employee when naturally interpreted.

EMPLOYER—Authority: Pastor; Christ; Satan; someone he or she resembles, in position, action, or character; actual employer when naturally interpreted.

EXPLOSION—Sudden: Sudden expansion or increase (as in "that church has had explosive growth since the new pastor arrived"); swift change; destruction.

EYEGLASSES—Magnify: Clarity; vision; enhance. If broken or lost = *Lack of vision*. Sunglasses = *Protect the vision;* shielded; screen. If negative = *Dark;* haughty; pride. Rose colour = *Looking for the best*. If negative = *Avoiding reality*.

EYES—Desire (Good or Evil): Covetousness; passion; lust; revelation; understanding; the windows of the soul. Winking = *Deceitfulness or cunning;* hiding true desire.

FACE—Heart: Sad; glad; mad; bad; etc.; the same as another person (when one looks into the mirror of another person's heart, he sees his own heart's reflection); before or against another person (as in "get out of my face!"); the actual person's face. False face = *Hiding truth;* trying to be someone else; hypocrite.

FACTORY—Production: Getting things done; the Kingdom of God; the Church; the "world"; the motions of sin. Idle factory = *Not busy;* not reaching full potential; natural workplace (when applicable).

FAIR—Festival: Feast; celebrate; socialize. Honest or dishonest judgment. Worldly; flesh.

FALCON—Hunter: Minister; leader; predator.

FALL—Ministry: A personal setback. Accident; repentance; end.

FALLING—Unsupported: Loss of support (financial, moral, public, etc.); trial; succumb; backsliding.

FAMILY—Relatives: Spiritual family or natural family.

FARM/FARMER—Labourer: Preacher; pastor; Christ; minister. Farm = *Field of labour:* an area of ministry; the Kingdom of God; the Church. The sower = *The Son of Man.* (See BARN and GARDENER)

FATHER—Authority: God; author; originator; source; inheritance; tradition; custom; Satan; natural father; spiritual covering

FATHER-IN-LAW—Law: An authoritative relationship based upon law (as in "Moses' Law" or "church government"); legalism; problem (authoritative) relationship; he may represent himself; teacher (spiritual).

FEATHERS—Covering: Spirit; safe place; a place of comfort; victory; weightless. Wet feathers = *Offense* (as in "madder then a wet hen"). Feather in your cap = *Symbolizing your victory;* award; reward.

FEET—Heart: Walk; way; journey; call to ministry; offence; stubborn (when unmovable); rebellion (when kicking); sin. Lame feet = *Sin/wound that affects the Christian life or ministry;* unbelief or error; doubt. Diseased feet = Offense (toward God or man). Barefoot = *Without preparation;* without understanding; without protection; without salvation; novice (as in "tenderfoot"); easily offended (as in tender feet).

FENCE—Boundaries: Barrier; obstacles; religious traditions; doctrines; inhibitions. Protection; safety net.

FIELD—World: God's work; harvest; opportunity; mixed multitude. Area; scope of authority; inheritance (mixed field).

FINGER—Work, Feeling, or Grip; Sensitivity; discernment; conviction. Work, as in HANDS. Pointing Finger = *Accusation;* direction (as in "he went that way"); instruction. Cutting off fingers = *Limiting authority or power.*

FIRE—Passion: Power; purify; cleanse; purge; refine; revival; anger; strife; desire; lust; zeal; trial; gossip. Fireplace = *Heart.*

FISH—Spirit or Soul: Person (good or bad); a person's character or motive (as in "something sure smells fishy about him").

FISHING—Hope: Witnessing; evangelizing; preaching. Expectation of harvest; patience.

FLASHLIGHT—Personal Revelation; understanding; guidance.

FLEA—Insignificant: Nuisance, irritant; elusive; small hindrance. Ineffective; lacking power or strength.

FLOOD—Overwhelm: Temptation; sin; judgment; depression; overcome. Disaster; cleansing or purging of evil.

FLOWERS—Glory: Gift; romance; springtime. Death; funeral; mourning. Bulb = *Blossom;* bloom; stages of growth.

FLY—Unclean: Corruption; demon; curse; nuisance.

FLYING—Soaring: Getting in the Spirit. Spiritual journey = *Spiritual high;* freedom.

FOG—Confusion or Temporary: Clouded issues or thoughts; obscurity; uncertainty. Protection; out of sight; covering.

FOOD—Work: Word of God; foundational truth; teaching. Spiritual food for babies in the Lord. Solid food = *Work of God;* teaching for the mature. Fat = *Excess*; abundance; fat in the Spirit; the anointing. Different foods will give further clarity:

MEAT—For the Mature.

MILK—For the Babe.

VEGETABLES—Healthy.

DESSERT—Treat or Finish.

FOOTBALL GAME—Ministry, Life, Work: Worship; team ministry; competition. Note different aspects of the game (run, pass, score, penalty etc.).—may provide clearer direction

FOREIGN—Alien: Not of God; of the flesh; demonic. Not of this world (therefore heavenly). Different culture; stranger. Foreigner = *Unrelated;* different; strange; unusual; doesn't fit.

FOREST—Hiding Place: A group of people standing together; confusion. (See TREE)

FORK IN THE RIVER OR ROAD—Time or Place of Decision or Change.

FOUNDATION—Base: Establish; stable or unstable (when shaky); the Gospel; sound doctrine; church government. Beginning or early in project or work of ministry.

FOX—Subtlety: Deception; cunning; a con man; false prophet; wicked leader; hidden sin or motive.

FRIEND—Self: The character or circumstance of one's friend reveals something about one's self. Sometimes one friend represents another (look for another with the same name, initials, hair colour, job, or trade, or one with similar traits, character, talents, personality, features, circumstances); actual friend when naturally interpreted.

FROG—Demon: Witchcraft; curse; evil words; (as in "casting a spell"); puffed up.

FRONT (FRONTYARD or FRONT PORCH)—Future: In the presence of; a prophecy of future events; immediately ahead. Sitting on porch = *Rest, comfort, patience;* waiting in expectation.

FRUIT—Productive: Results; glory; of ministry life.

GARBAGE (DUMP)—Rejected: Filth; hell; evil; vile; corruption. A place to leave your past sins or relationships that are not productive.

GARDENER—The Lord: Pastor, the enemy. Working with; caring for our life or our mind or heart or thoughts.

GAS FUMES—Deception: Deceiving spirit; evil motive; leaking information; envy; false accusations; slander; danger.

GASOLINE—Fuel: Prayer; gossip; energy; power.

GIANT—Strongman: Champion; challenge; obstacle; trouble; spiritual warfare; hindrance; battle; foe or opponent; demonic stronghold.

GLOVES—Protection: Safe; careful. White gloves = *Clean;* inspection; keeping clean hands; holy hands. Black or dirty gloves = *Evil works;* sin, secret sin; evil intention.

GOAT—Sinner: Unbelief; stubborn; unyielding; strife; argumentative; negative person; scapegoat (blamed for another's wrongdoing). Sheep and goats = *Mingled field*.

GOLD—Glory or wisdom: Truth; something precious; righteous; glory of God. Self-glorification; greed; provision; power.

GOLF—Worship: Competition; individual sport; challenging field of ministry. For more clarification note aspects of game: Teeing off (driving) = *Start*. Holing out = *Finish*. Penalty = *Out of bounds;* etc.

GOVERNOR—Ruler: Christ; authority; covering (spiritual or natural).

GRANDCHILD—Heir: Oneself; inherited blessing or iniquity; one's spiritual legacy; actual grandchild when naturally interpreted. Generational blessing or curse.

GRANDMOTHER—Past: Spiritual inheritance (good or evil). Self-examination for inherited traits, faults, or sins. Could be your mother or herself in the natural.

GRANDFATHER—Past: Spiritual inheritance (good or evil). Spiritual authority and wisdom or tradition. Self-examination for inherited traits, faults, or sins. Could be your father or himself in the natural.

GRAPES—Fruit: The Spirit of promise; fruit of the Spirit; promise of wrath.

GRASS—Flesh: The Word of God. High grass = *Needing care;* freedom or liberty. Temporary; here today, gone tomorrow.

DRIED GRASS—Death: Repentance; spiritual drought.

GREEN GRASS—Life: Self-renewal.

MOWED GRASS—Chastisement: Repentance; correction; crucifying flesh. Sickness; financial need or distress; emotional and mental depression or anguish. Preparation for blessing or revival (the rain falls on the mowed grass).

GRASSHOPPER—Smallness of Size: Multitude to destroy. Locust = *Devourer;* pestilence; plague.

GRAVEL PIT/QUARRY—Source: The Word of God; abundant supply. Redemption; reclaiming.

GRAVEL ROAD—Way: God's Word and way. For further clarification, note conditions of the road: rocky, muddy, dusty, narrow, etc.

GRAVEYARD—Hidden: Out of the past; curse; evil inheritance; hypocrisy; death; demon; witchcraft; fear.

GREEN—Life: Mortal; flesh; carnal; envy; inexperienced; immature; renewal.

GREY—Not Defined: Unclear (as in "the grey area between right and wrong"); vague; not specific; hazy; deceived; deception; hidden; crafty; false doctrine. Heaviness; depressing; double-minded.

GREY HAIR—Wisdom: Age; aging.

GROOM—The Lord: Husband; new covenant relationship. Natural marriage when naturally interpreted.

GROUND FLOOR—First floor: Starting or young work; entry- level opportunity; foundation.

GUNS/BULLETS—Words: Accusations; slander; gossip; power. Broken or inoperative gun = *Without authority or ability or power.* For further clarity, the size, style, and colour of the gun will tell you more about the purpose and the power. Examples: Starter pistol = *Start the race*. Double-barrel shotgun = *Double blessing, anointing, power, or authority*. Powerful couple in ministry.

HAIL—Judgment: Punishment; destruction; bombardment; spiritual attack.

HAIR—Covering: Covenant; humanity; the old (sinful) nature; tradition; power; strength. Long-haired man = *Defiance;* rebellion. Long-haired woman = *Glory;* beauty. Letting hair down = *Informal;* relaxed; intimate. Shaving = *Putting away the filthiness or nature of the flesh*. Hair growing back out = *Restoration;* restoring the covenant or strength.

HAIRCUT—Putting Away Tradition or Bad Habits: Repenting of bad attitudes. Removing or breaking covenants or religious traditions. Repentance; correction.

HAMMER—Force: Word of God; preaching; evil words; destruction. Building; strengthening; shaping.

HANDS—Works: Deeds (good or evil); labour; service; idolatry; spiritual warfare. Raised hands = *Worship;* surrender. Clenched fist = *Fighting or anger*. Two people shaking hands = *Covenant;* agreement. Hands trembling = *Weakness or fear*. Hands outstretched, palms up = *Helplessness*. Hands covering face = *Grief;* guilt; shame; laughter. (Other self-explanatory uses of hands include: waving good-bye; begging; prayer (clasped together); calling someone to "come" or to "follow.")

HARLOT—Seduction: The worldly church; adultery; fornication; temptation; snare; unclean person.

HAT—Covering: Protection; thought; attitude; diversity (as in "wearing many different hats"). Type of hat can help clarify purpose or authority,eg., ball cap, headdress.

HAWK—Predator: Sorcerer; evil spirit; leader; scavenger; a person who is for war.

HAY—To Bundle: Prepare (as in "make hay while the sun shines"); harvest; gather people; carnality; death.

HEAD—Authority: God; Christ; covering; government; husband; pastor; employer; power; first in order.

HEAT—Power: Zeal; passion. Turn up the heat = *Increase the power*.

HELICOPTER—Ministry: Individual; the Church; versatile; small traveling ministry; short-term ministry trips. Hovering = *No forward motion*; stationary; lack of progress.

HEN—Protection: Gossip.

HIGHWAY—Way: The Christian faith; truth; way of life; way of error. Under construction = *In preparation;* change; hindrance. Crossroads = *Change of direction*; place of decision. Type of road or traffic conditions can provide further insight.

HIPS (LOINS)—Mind: Truth; joint; reproduction.

HOG—Unclean: Unkempt; lazy; backslidden.

HOMOSEXUAL ACTS—Rebellion:Unnatural; disobedience; wives not obeying their husbands; husbands not bearing their responsibility of headship properly (wimp); ungodly relationships or covenants.

HONEY—Power: Holy Spirit anointing and enlightenment; wisdom; knowledge; pleasant experience.

HORNET—Affliction: Stinging, biting words; slander; strife; curse (because of sin); persecution; trouble; offense; demonic spirits.

HORNS—Authority: Power; ability; king; anointing.

HORSE—Work: Flesh; age; strength; vehicle (as in "horse and rider"); grace.

BLACK HORSE—Famine: Bad times; evil.

RED HORSE—Persecution: Anger; danger; opposition.

KICKING/LIFTING HEEL—Threatening: Betrayal; rebellion; persecution.

QUARTER HORSE—Strong: Good times; fast; agility.

HOSPITAL—Care: Church; place of healing; mercy; persons who are wounded or sick; retreat center.

HOTEL—Public Place for Rest or Business: Church; public gathering; travel; business travel.

HOURGLASS—Running Out of Time: Last days; hurry.

HOUSE—Person, Family or Individual: Church. Naturally interpreted, it means a dwelling place. Heart; ministry; safe place; identity; roots. Different rooms, parts, and condition of the house can have specific meaning:

NEW HOUSE—New Life (as in salvation): Change; revival; new move (natural or spiritual).

OLD HOUSE—Past: Inheritance, e.g., one's grandfather's or grandmother's religion, ways, or temperament; established tradition. In bad condition = *Our sins or the sins of our forefathers.* Needing revival (when in need of repair or remodeling); untended; neglect; unusable; ruin.

ATTIC—Memories: Strange; attitude; mind.

BASEMENT—Past: Hidden; stored. Foundation level.

BATHROOM—Deliverance or Cleansing: Prayer of repentance.

BEDROOM—Rest: Place of intimacy; private place.

DOORS—Authority: Way; avenue.

FAMILY ROOM—Reveal: Fellowship; comfortable; casual; relax.

FIREPLACE—Heart.

KITCHEN—Heart.

LIVING ROOM—Formal: Hospitality; revealed; truth.

ROOF—Covering: Pastor; protection.

WINDOWS—Revealed: Vision; prophecy; revelation.

HOUSE TRAILER—Temporary: Place; situation; relationship.

HUNTING—Evangelizing: Seeking; provision; work.

HUSBAND—Authority: God or Christ; pastor; partner; natural husband; Satan, if evil or mean.

ICE—Danger: Warning; slippery condition, solid; frozen in place spiritually.

INDIAN—First: Firstborn; chief; fierce; savvy; native; rebellion; warrior.

INSURANCE—Faith: Protection; prepared; safe; covered; confidence; future provision for one's family.

INTERSECTION—Crossroad: Decision; hindrance; proceed with care.

IRON—Strength: Powerful; invincible; stronghold; stubborn.

IRONING—Change: Sanctification; instruction in righteousness; God's discipline; correction; repentance; working out problem relationships; reconciliation.

JESTER—Fool: Clown; joy; entertainment; worldly.

JEWELRY—Treasure: Desire; precious; God's gifts; idolatry; self-glorification; pride; precious person; gifted person; truth.

JOGGING—Staying in condition: Working; striving; preparing.

JUDGE—Authority: God; conscience; minister; Satan, if evil authority.

JUNKYARD—Ruined: Waste; wrecked; lost souls; corruption.

KANGAROO—To Jump: Predisposition; hopping around; jump to a conclusion; Australia. Pouch = *Safe place.*

KEY—Authority: Power; wisdom; understanding; ability; important or indispensable. Keystone or cornerstone = *Christ.*

KICKING—Attack: Rebellion; conflict.

KISS—Agreement: Covenant; enticement; betrayal; covenant breaker; deception; seduction; friend; relationship; intimacy.

KITCHEN—Heart: Intent; motive; plans; passion; preparation; ambition; affliction.

KNEES—Submission: Obey; worship; serve; stubborn; unyielding; prayer; surrender; begging.

KNIVES—Words: Revelation; truth; sharp or angry rebuke; accusations; gossip.

LADDER—Ascend or Descend: Enable; way of escape; way of entrance. Steps upward = *Promotion*. Steps downward = *Demotion;* trial.

LAMB—Jesus: Young believer; innocence; naive.

LAWYER—Advocate: Holy Spirit; Christ; defender of freedom; helper; counselor; defense; authority; minister; intercessor; a legalistic minister; devil's advocate; accuser.

LEAVEN—Spirit (Good or Evil): Attitude; sin; false doctrine; hypocrisy; self-justification; self-righteousness; self-importance; anger; pride, zeal.

LEAVES—Words or healing: Covering; covenant; testimony; temporary; self-justification.

LEFT—Spiritual: Weakness (of man); God's strength or ability demonstrated through man's weakness; rejection. Left Turn = *Spiritual change*.

LEGS—Support: Spirit; strength; work stable. Legs on a table = *Support;* stability; in covenant.

LEMON—Fruit: Bitter; sour; bad deal; crabby.

LEOPARD—Powerful Leader: Predator; permanent; unchanging evil person; danger.

LIBRARY—Knowledge: Education; learning; research; school; teaching ministry; doctrine; legalistic.

LICE—Shame: Guilt; accusation; affliction; nuisance, problem with covering.

LICENSE—Authority: Approval; registered; government. To permit; to allow.

LIGHT—Manifest: Revealed; exposed. Turning the lights out = *Closing;* finish; end.

LIGHTNING—Power: Instant miracle; judgment; destruction; knowledge.

LION—Christ: King; regal; bold; power; Satan; religious tradition; destroying spirit.

LIPS—Words: Seduction; speech.

LIVING ROOM—Revealed: Everyday or current affairs; that which is manifest; truth exposed.

LIZARD/SALAMANDER—Early Stages: Immature; Leviathan spirit; worldly.

LOST—Lose: Confused; in need of direction; lacking; unsaved; soul lost through sin. Lost = *Truth lost through tradition;* gift lost through neglect. Found = *Revelations or gifts received from God;* receiving revelation knowledge.

LUMBER—Building Project: Building materials; temporary; temporal; carnal.

MAGGOT—Corruption: Filthiness of the flesh; evil; rot; spoil; devourer.

MAN—Angel, Oneself, or Demon: God's messenger; person with evil intent; danger. Kind Stranger = *Jesus;* a minister of mercy; helper; Holy Spirit.

MAP—Directions: Word of God; correction; advice; location.

MARRIAGE—Covenant: The Church as the Bride of Christ; agreement; joined. Sexual intimacy = *One in agreement.* Interruption of intimacy = *Interference or trouble in marriage or covenant relationship.*

MECHANIC—Minister: Christ; prophet; pastor; counselor; need for adjustment in theology, attitude, relationship, etc. Mechanic's tools = *Word of God;* gifts of the Spirit; wisdom and knowledge.

MEDICINE—Healing: Direction; correction; prescription; counselling.

MICE—Devourer: Curse; plague; timid.

MICROPHONE—Voice: Authority; ministry; influence; amplify; increase, preach.

MICROSCOPE—Examine: Close examination; self-examination.

MICROWAVE OVEN—Instant: Quick work; sudden; impatience; convenience.

MILK—A Work of Service: Foundational teaching; feeding or nurturing.

MIRROR—Reflection: Looking at oneself; looking back; memory; past; vanity.

MISCARRIAGE—Abort: Failure; loss; repentance; unjust judgment.

MISSILE—Strong Attack: Power; spiritual warfare.

MONEY—Power: Provision; wealth; natural talents and skills; spiritual riches; power; authority; covetousness.

MONKEY—Foolishness: Mischief; dishonesty; addiction.

MOON—To Rule: To manifest the works of darkness; occult; false worship; persecution.

MOTEL—Church/Ministry: Housing multiple ministries; temporary location, travel, rest.

MOTH—Deterioration: Loss through deceit; secret or undetected trouble; corruption; destructive power; chastisement.

MOTHER—Source: Church; spiritual or natural mother; love; kindness. Mother-in-law= *Legalistic church;* meddler; trouble; she may represent herself.

MOTOR—Power: Motive; motivation; anointing; spirit; heart.

MOTORCYCLE—Personal Ministry: Independence; rebellion; selfish; pride; swift progress.

MOUNTAIN—Place of Prayer: Meditation; victory and revelation; obstacle; difficulty; challenge; kingdom (nation).

MOVIE—Message: Announcement. Content and characters will bring further clarity.

MOVING—Change: Can be literal; may represent church change, career or job change. A changing season or assignment; can be spiritual or natural.

MUDDY ROAD, PATH, OR RIVER—Flesh: Man's way; lust; passion; temptation; offense; strife; sin; need for caution; impassable; difficulty caused by the weakness of the flesh.

MULE—Stubborn: Self-willed; tenacious; strong; also unbelief.

MUSEUM—Heritage: Past; tradition; church or ministry that is not active or moving forward.

MUSIC—Worship: Of God; of idols (idolatry); activity or action that proceeds from the heart. Playing Instruments = *Prophesying*; ministering in the gifts of the Spirit; worshiping.

NAILS—Words: Word of God or man; wisdom; vows; covenant; fasten; steadfast; permanent; unmovable; unchangeable; secure.

NAME—Identity: Authority; reputation; the name's meaning; a person with the same initials; a different person with the same name or similar personality, nature, character, or reputation; the actual person in the dream.

NATION—Characteristic: That for which the people are known, such as food or culture; personal memories of travel; call to; intercession for.

NECK—Will: Self-willed; stubborn; unbelief; authority; rule.

NEWSPAPER—Announcement: Important event; public exposure; news; prophecy; gossip.

NIGHT—Darkness: Ignorance; hidden; unknown course of action; sin; power of evil.

NOISE—Annoyance: Interference; disturbance; destruction. Certain sounds can bring more clarity.

NORTH—Spiritual: Judgment; Heaven or heavenly; spiritual warfare ("as in taking your inheritance"); Canada.

NORTHERN LIGHTS—Canada: Arctic; splendour; direction.

NOSE—Busybody or Discern: Nosy; close victory or loss ("by a nose"); meddling; strife; smell.

NOSEBLEED—Strife: Trouble.

NUDITY—Uncovered or Flesh: Self-justification and self-righteousness, impure; ashamed; stubborn; temptation; lust; seduction; exhibitionism; innocence; vulnerable; open (revealed); truth; honest; nature. Without spiritual covering.

NUTS AND BOLTS—Essential: Bottom line; indispensable; wisdom; to fasten; secure; unmovable; unyielding.

OIL—Anointing: Holy Spirit; healing; lubricate; loosen; ease; maintain. Dirty Oil = *Unclean spirit;* hate; lust; seduction; deception; slick; danger.

OLD MAN—Carnal (as in "put off the old man"): Wisdom (especially if he is white headed); weak; respect; tradition.

ONE'S CHILDREN—Oneself or Themselves: Character or behaviour reveals something about oneself (or something about one's child if the dream is to be naturally interpreted). Sometimes children gathered together from different families from one's own church represent the church members.

ORANGE—Danger: Great jeopardy; harm. Fiery orange = *Power;* force; energy; energetic; danger; intense.

OVEN—Heart: Heat of passion; one's imagination "cooking up" good or evil; meditation; judgment.

OVERSLEEP—Late: Missing an appointment or opportunity.

OWL—Circumspect (Looking Around): Wisdom; demon; curse.

PAINTING—Covering: Regenerate; remodel; renovate; love; covering up sin; doctrine; truth or deception. Artist's painting = *Words;* illustrative message; eloquent; humorous; articulate; creative. Colours, subjects, and scenes bring further revelation and clarity.

PARACHUTING—Leave: Bail out; escape; flee; saved. Parachute = *God's promises;* salvation; faith; safety net; insurance.

PARASITES—Ticks, Termites, Leeches: People or circumstances or things that distract, take energy or life from a person, ministry, or work; nuisance; hindrance; pest.

PARK—Rest: Peace; God's blessing; God's provision; leisure; vagrancy.

PARROT—Mimic: Copy; mock; repeat. Prophet of God or false prophet.

PASTOR—Shepherd: Spouse; protection; God; spiritual authority; covering; minister; Satan, when evil.

PATH—Way: Life; private walk with God; gospel; salvation; error; misjudgement.

PEN/PENCIL—Tongue: Indelible words; covenant; agreement; contract; vow; publish; record; permanent; unforgettable; gossip.

PERFUME—Influence: Seduction; enticement; temptation; persuasion; gossip; cover up evil.

PICKUP TRUCK—Work: Personal ministry or natural work.

PICTURE—Memory: Conscience; past experience; circumstance; imagination; a message within itself (as in "a picture is worth a thousand words"). Picture taken with an important person = *Honour*; promotion. Unusual picture frame = *Attitude* (as in "a peculiar frame of mind"); Old or antique frame = *Time or age.*

PIE—Whole: Business endeavours; part of the action. Fruit pie = *Fruit;* work of service.

PIG—Unclean Spirit: Ignorant; sexual sin; dirty; rude; glutton; unbeliever; lazy.

PILLS—Remedy: Medication; drugs; influence; bitter.

PILOT—Minister: Traveling minister; daring.

PINEAPPLE—Fruit: Fruitful; prosperity; Hawaii.

PINK—Flesh: Sensual; sensuous; immoral; moral; chaste; a baby girl.

PIPE—Dignified: Pride.

PLATFORM—Stage: Entertain; preach; highlight; leadership opportunity; launch; start.

PLAY—Worship: Idolatry; covetousness; spiritual warfare; striving; competition. Different games and aspects of games or sports will give further revelation, meaning, and clarity.

POLICE—Authority: Natural or spiritual authority, good or evil; protection; angels or demons; an enforcer of a curse of the law.

POND—Refreshing: Natural; peaceful; place to evangelize (fish).

POOL—Spiritual place: Church; ministry; home, family; refreshing or revival center; God's blessings. Dirty or dry pool or pond = *Corrupt or destitute spiritual condition*; backslidden; unclean; hidden sin or heart condition. Water stirring = *Healing*; spiritual movement or activity.

PORCH—Protection: Past; exposed; revealed. Front porch = *Future*. Side porch = *Current*. Back porch = *Past*.

POSTAGE STAMP—Seal: Authority; authorization.

POT/PAN/BOWL/PLATE—Vessel: Doctrine; tradition; truth or person.

PREACHER—Messenger: God's representative; spiritual authority (good or evil) God or Satan. Pastor's Wife = *Church or member;* covenant partner.

PREGNANCY—In Process: Sin or righteousness in process; desire; anticipation; expectancy; promise on the way. Labour pains = *Trials*; travail; soon.

PRISON—Bondage: Strong emotion; addiction; destructive behaviours and habits.

PRISONERS—Lost Souls: Stubborn sinners; persecuted saints; person in bondage or need of deliverance.

PUMPKIN—Witchcraft: Deception; snare; witch; trick.

PURPLE—Royal: Rule (good or evil); majestic; noble.

PURSE—Treasure: Heart; personal identity; precious; valuable. When empty = *Spiritually bankrupt.*

RABBIT—Increase: Fast growth; multiplication.

RACCOON—Mischief: Night raider; rascal; thief; bandit; deceitful.

RADIO—Unceasing: Continuous; contentious; unbelieving; tradition; news; the Gospel being broadcast; unrelenting; sound; signals. Truth; error; witness.

RAFT—Adrift: Without direction; aimless; powerless; makeshift.

RAILING ON STAIRS OR PORCH—Steady: Safety; barrier; boundary; protection.

RAILROAD TRACK—Tradition: Unchanging; habit; stubborn; Gospel; caution; danger; hindrance; parallel; unending works. Way or road of revival.

RAIN—Life: Revival; Holy Spirit; Word of God; depression; trial; disappointment.

RAINBOW—Covenant: Promise; good; protection.

RAPE—Violation: Abuse of authority; forcing one's will on another; hate; desire for revenge; murder.

RAPTURE—Revival: Spiritual awakening; warning of unpreparedness if left behind; suddenly; unexpected rescue.

RAT—Unclean: Wicked person; devourer; plague; betrayer. (See MICE)

REARVIEW MIRROR—Legalism; Looking back; paranoia.

RED— Passion: Emotion; anger; hatred; lust; sin; enthusiasm; zeal.

REED—Weak: A spiritually weak person; opposition that comes through the weakness of the flesh; affliction.

REFRIGERATOR—Heart: Motive; attitude; thoughts. Stored food = *Memories stored in the heart.* Spoiled food = *Harbouring a grudge;* unclean thoughts or desires.

REPAIR SHOP—Ministry of Restoration: Restoration for ministries or individuals. Body shop = *Place where people's characters and lives are moulded in preparation for ministry.*

RESTAURANT—Church: Ministry; teaching; meeting place; public; gathering place.

RIGHT—Natural: Authority; power; the strength of man (flesh) or the power of God revealed through flesh; accepted.

RIGHT TURN—Natural Change: Power or strength of man; correct.

RING—Covenant: Authority; eternity; unending; prestige. Wedding Ring = *Covenant.* Engagement Ring = *Promise.*

RIVER—Spirit or Life (the Spirit of God, the spirit of man, or the world): Sin; wickedness; judgment; righteousness; trial. Deep, wide, or muddy river = *Difficulty;* obstacle; impassable; incomprehensible.

DRY RIVERBED—Barren: Tradition; backslidden condition; repented (as when Israel obeyed and crossed the Jordan on dry ground after their forefathers refused to go in and possess the land).

ROACHES—Unclean spirit: Uncleanness; infestation; plague; hidden sin.

ROAD—Way: Christian life or walk. Types of road condition can provide added insight.

ROBBERY—Theft: Stealing promise, blessing, or provision.

ROCKET—Power: Powerful ministry; swift progress; swift destruction; sudden, unexpected attack; war.

ROCKING CHAIR—Past Memories: Meditation; retirement; rest.

ROLLER COASTER—Unstable: Emotional instability; unfaithfulness; wavering; manic-depressive; bipolar; depression; trials; excitement.

ROLLER SKATES—Speed: Fast; swift advancement or progress; skillful.

ROOF—Covering: Protection; mind; thought; oversight; government or covenant (good or evil); Holy Spirit.

ROOFTOP—Revealed: Manifest.

ROOSTER— Boasting: Bragging; proud.

ROOT—Attitude: Hidden sin; right and wrong attitudes or values; hidden cause or source; giving strength and stability.

ROPE/CORD—Bondage: Sin; covenant; vow; hindrances; rescue; salvation.

ROSE—Romance: Love; courtship. Red rose = *Passion*. Yellow rose garden = *Marriage counseling*.

ROUND (SHAPE)—Spiritual: Grace; mercy; compassion; forgiveness; approximate; unending; continuous work.

ROWBOAT—Small Ministry or Life: Man's power; striving.

ROWING—Work: Working out life's problems; earnest prayer; spiritual labour. (See BICYCLE)

RUG—Covering: Covenant; Holy Spirit; deception or covering things up.

RUNNING—Striving: Working out one's salvation; faith; haste; trial.

RUT—Tradition: Habit; addiction.

SABOTAGE—Hindrance: Demonic spirits working against you, hindering God's will or fulfillment for your life.

SALT—Seasoning or Preservative: Covenant; acceptable; memorial; rejected.

SALTWATER—Spirit of the World: Unclean; source of evil.

SAND—Flesh: Improper foundation; weakness; weariness; drudgery; hindrance. (See SEACOAST)

SCALES—Justice: Judgment; balance; fair; true; wisdom; law.

SCHOOL— Teaching or Learning: Church; people or work; teaching ministry; training.

SCHOOL BUS—Church: School; youth group; children's ministry.

SCORPION—Sin Nature: Lust of the flesh; temptation; deception; accusation; destruction; danger; deadly.

SEA—Humanity: People; nations; gentiles; barrier.

SEACOAST—Boundary: Heart or soul; flesh; limitations.

SEAL—Authority; closed; protected; final. Specialized military unit (Navy SEALS) = *Undercover*; special tactics; elite; spiritual warfare.

SEAT BELT—Security: Safety; assurance. Unfastened = *Unsafe* (lack of prayer, commitment, attention to detail; rebellion or error.).

SEED—Word: Word of God; saints; faith; word of man; revealing the heart; Christ; fullness of iniquity. Offering; multiplication; preparation for and expectation of the harvest; duplication; anointing.

SEESAW/TEETER-TOTTER—Balance: Up and down; back and forth; try; double-minded; innocent.

SEWAGE—Corruption: Filthiness of the flesh; sin; evil; corrupt authority; abuse of authority; waste.

SEWING—Joining: Union; reunion; counseling; reconciliation.

SEX—Agreement: Covenant; unity; taken advantage of or "used"; abuse of authority. When naturally interpreted = *Love or fornication*. Masturbation = *Self-gratification;* inordinate self-love; selfishness; wasting your seed. Genitals = *Secret;* private matter; shame.

SHAVING—Cleansing: Repentance.

SHEEP—Innocent: Saints; unsaved persons; easily led; not self-directed; children of God; members of a church. Lamb = *Sacrifice*.

SHIP—Life or Ministry: Vessel. Type and size of ship will give more clarity (e.g.,ocean liner, party boat, tugboat, barge).

SHIRT—Covering or Protection: Heart = *Righteousness or sin*. Without a shirt = *Self-righteousness* (self-justification); legalism; shame; temptation; seduction, lust of the flesh.

SHOES/BOOTS—Words: Gospel; covenant; preparation. New shoes = *New ministry or way of life*. House slippers = *Self-examination*. Loafers = *Casual;* at ease; unconcern; hypocrisy; loafing. Combat or heavy boots = *Spiritual warfare*. Steel-toed boots = *Protection*. (See FEET)

SHOULDERS—Support: Bearer; government; authority; responsibility; stubborn. Broad shoulders = *Strength;* consolation. Drooped shoulders = *Tired;* overburdened; discouraged; hopelessness. Bare female shoulders = *Seduction;* temptation; witchcraft.

SHOVEL—Tongue: Prayer; confession; gossip; slander; dig; search; inquire.

SHOWER—Cleansing: Repentance; deliverance; refreshing; revival.

SIGN—Directions: Stop sign = *Stop*. Yield sign = *Yield*. Detour sign = *Change of Direction.* Intersection sign= *Decision or change.* Keep off the grass = *Give no man offence;* boundary; limit.

SILVER—Knowledge: Wealth; power; worldly; redemption; revelation knowledge.

SISTER—Self: Natural or spiritual sister; someone she reminds you of (same name, initials, character, etc.) the Church.

SISTER-IN-LAW—Someone she reminds you of or she may represent her family, herself, or woman minister or church. Other possibilities are: Your brother's wife = *Spiritual or natural.*

SKATEBOARD—Balance: Skillful maneuvering; skillful ministry; risky; danger; fast; moving in the Spirit; free-spirited.

SKIING (WATER or SNOW SKIING)—Faith: Supported by God's power through faith; fast progress. Flowing in the Spirit; worshiping.

SKIRT—Covering: Natural or spiritual; protection; covering shame or embarrassment; grace. (See CLOTHING)

SLEEP—Unconscious: Unaware; hidden or covered; ignorant; danger; death; rest; laziness.

SLOTHFUL—Lazy: Lethargic; lifeless; slow; without energy or motive; aimless.

SMILE—Friendly: Kindness; benevolent; greeting; goodwill; without offense; seduction.

SMOKE—Manifest Presence: Evidence (as in "where there's smoke, there's fire"); glory of God; prayer; lying or boasting; offense; temporary; cover-up.

SMOKE DETECTOR—Alarm: Protection; safety. When sounding = *Warning;* impending danger.

SMOKING—Pride: Smoking cigarettes = *Pride or bitterness;* bitter memories; offense; unforgiving; envy; jealousy; self-righteousness. Smoking a cigar = *Haughty;* arrogant; boastful. Smoking a pipe = *Intellectual;* pride; dignitary.

SNAKE—Curse: Demon; deception; threat; danger; hatred; slander; critical spirit; witchcraft. Fangs = *Evil intent*; danger. Rattles = *Words*; threats; warning; alarm.

SNOW—Word: White snow = *Pure*; grace; covered; unrevealed; unfulfilled. Dirty snow = *Impure*. Snowdrift = *Barrier*; hindrance; opposition; snare.

SNOWSHOES—Faith: Walking in the Spirit; supported by faith in the Word of God.

SOAP—Cleansing: Conviction; forgiveness; prayer; repentance.

SOCKS—Covering (Same as UNDERGARMENTS): Socks without shoes = *Without full preparation*. White socks = *Pure heart*. Black or dirty socks = *Impure heart*.

SOLDIER—Warfare: Spiritual warfare; angel (protection); demon (accuser or opponent): persecution. (See GUNS/BULLETS)
SON—Spiritual or Natural Son: One with same or similar name, initials, characteristics, or career; oneself.

SOUTH—Natural: World; sin; temptation; trial; flesh; corruption; deception or the natural south in direction; Mexico, south of the border.

SPORTING EVENTS—Ministry Work in Progress: Competition; striving for victory; team concept. If spectator = *Watching or observing some event of life or ministry*; unfolding. Excited for = *Encouraging or cheering one on*. Events within the event = *Penalty*; score; equipment failure. Coach = *Teacher*; helper.

SPIDER (WEB)—Evil: Sin; deception; false doctrine; temptation; snare; lies; entanglement; setting a trap.

BLACK WIDOW—Danger: Great danger; deadly; evil; slander.

SPRING—(New) Beginning: Revival; fresh start; renewal; forward; regeneration; salvation; refreshing. Start of a church ministry or season.

SQUARE (SHAPE)—Legalistic: Religious or religion (speaking the truth without love); no mercy; hard or harsh; of the world; box or limit.

STAIRS—Promotion: Ambition (self-promotion); procedure. Stairs going down = *Demotion;* backslide; failure. Guardrail = *Safety;* precaution; warning to be careful.

STAR—Person: Christian; apostle; saint; preacher; minister; angel; leader or role model; hero or movie star.

STONE—Word: Building block; individual church member; testimony; person; precept; condemnation; accusation; persecution; punishment.

STORK—Expectant: New birth; new baby; new experience; that which is forthcoming; delivery of blessings or message or promise.

STORM—Disturbance: Change; spiritual warfare; judgment; sudden calamity or destruction; trial; persecution; opposition; witchcraft. White storm = *God's power;* revival.

STOVE—Something Cooking: Thought; imagination; heart.

STRAIGHT—Spiritual Progression: Righteousness; walking in alignment; sound doctrine.

STREET—Way: Christian walk; size of construction and other factors will help to determine meaning.

STUMBLE—Fail: Sin; backslide; mistake; become deceived; to be overcome; obstacle; ignorance.

STUMP—A Person: Life or ministry that has been cut down; no life; memory of what once was; repentance; judgment.

SUGAR—Sweetener: Power; anointing; pleasant experience.

SUICIDE—Self-destruction: Self-hatred; grief; remorse; foolish action; selfish; error; self-inflicted; judgment.

SUITCASE—Personal: Heart; travel; move; temporary (as in "living out of a suitcase").

SUMMER—Growing Season: Turning up the heat; long days; slow days; trial; heat of affliction. (See SUN)

SUN—God: Light; goodness; affliction; persecution; trial; god of this world; idol worship.

SWEEPING—Cleaning: Repentance; change (as in "a sweeping change"); removing obstacles; rebuking evildoers; all, encompassing move; wide turn; risky decision.

SWIMMING—Spiritual: Serving God; worshiping; operating in the gifts of the Spirit; prophesying. Working or striving; competition when appropriate.

SWINE—Unclean: Selfish; backslider; unbeliever; glutton; fornicator; hypocrite; idolater.

SWING—Peaceful: Rest; quietness; romance; fellowship. Swinging high (park swing) = *Danger;* immorality; infidelity; risky thrill seeking; double-minded; back and forth.

SWORD—Sharp Words: Word of God; weapon of honour; critical words; duel or personal attack or conflict; evil intent; threat; strife; war; persecution.

TABLE—Communion: Agreement; covenant; conference; provision. Under the table = *Deceitful dealings;* hidden motives; evil intent.

TAIL—Last in Time, Rank or Importance: That which follows; afterward; least. Wagging tail = *Friendly*. Tucked tail = *Guilt*; shame; cowardly.

TAN—Death: Dull; without power or purpose.

TAR—Covering: Repair; patch bitterness; offense; hatred; grudge.

TASTING—Experience: Discern; try; test; judge.

TEA—Refreshing: Grace; good news; salvation; time of refreshing; revival. English; proper; break; fellowship or rest.

TEARS—Grief: Sorrow; anguish; repentance; prayer; judgment; joy; cleansing.

TEETER-TOTTER—Up and Down: Unstable; unsure; procrastinator; not able to make decisions.

TEETH—Experience: Work; meditate (as in "to chew up"). Brushing Teeth = *Cleaning one's thoughts or words*; meditation. Animal Teeth (when an animal in the dream bares its teeth) = *Danger*.

BABY TEETH—Immaturity: Without experience; without wisdom or knowledge; innocent.

FALSETEETH—False Doctrine/False Wisdom or Knowledge: Worldly logic; tradition; error. Wisdom or knowledge gained through experience or previous failures; logical reasoning; without wisdom.

TELEPHONE—Communication: Prayer; message from God;

counsel; gossip. Phone inoperative or busy = *Prayer hindered;* interference; lack of revelation or prayer; business.

TELESCOPE—Future: Prophetic vision of the future; at a distance; far away in time.

TELEVISION—Vision: Message; prophecy; preaching; news; evil influence; wickedness.

TENNIS GAME—Worship: Play; sports; individual ministry. Back and forth (depending which side of the net the ball is on); decision (as in "the ball is in your court)."

TERMITES—Corruption: Hidden destruction; secret sin; deception; demon spirits.

TEST (EXAM)—Trial: Examination; opportunity for promotion; God could be testing you; difficult season; stretching; temptation.

THIEF—Hidden: Deceiver, deception; fraud; destruction; Satan; evil intent; works of the flesh; unexpected loss.

THIGH—Flesh: The natural man; works of the flesh; lust; seduction; power; strength of man.

THORNS—Hindrance: Gossip; evil circumstance; persecution; cares of this life; curse.

THUMB—Grip: Hold; victory (as in "thumbs up").

THUNDER—Power: Signs; wonders; powerful preaching; a voice for change. Dispensational change; a warning of impending judgment or trouble.

TICK—Hidden: Oblivious of one's true self; hidden unclean spirit; parasite; pest.

TIGER/LEOPARD—Danger: Powerful minister; evil; dangerous person.

TIME/TIMING—Clock: Time. If sense of pressure = *Decision*. Specific numbers will further help clarify meaning.

THIRD HOUR—Nine o'clock.

SIXTH HOUR—Noon.

ELEVENTH HOUR—Final hour; last days ministry.

HIGH NOON—Time of Confrontation; important encounter; time to bring the fullness of government or authority; joining together.

TIN—Dross: Waste; worthless; cheap; purification; hot. Tin roof = *Covering*.

TIRES—Spirit: Life; prayer; work on the move. Deflated/flat tire = *Discouragement;* dismay; hindrance; lack of prayer; spiritual condition.

TITLE/DEED—Ownership: Authorization; possession; authority; rule; government; approval.

TOOLS—Gifts: Talents; ability; enablement; works; help.

TONGUE—Words: Weapon; gossip; rebellion (untamed).

TRACTOR (FARM)—Powerful work: Preaching; ploughing; church or ministry; preparing for the harvest; making progress.

TRACTOR-TRAILER—Large burden: Ministry; powerful and/or large work; the Church. Tractor-trailer without trailer = *Free;* liberated in or with power; no responsibility.

TRACK—Unending Work: On track or on target; in proper alignment; course set; parallel or similar work.

TRAIN—Continuous: Unceasing work; the Church; revival; fast.

TRAIN STATION—Revival church or ministry center: Place of unending work of God; a temporary location or stop along the way; rest; a resting place in your particular ministry or life; waiting; place to make a connection.

TRANSMISSION—Change: Steps; change of direction; change of purpose or intensity of ministry; transformation.

TREE(S)—Person or Covering: Leader; pick up the pace; life; shelter; false worship; evil influence. Oak tree = *Strong shelter;* promise fulfilled; long-lasting work; life; multiplication. Willow tree = *Sorrow;* sadness; crying; weeping; placed for revival (planted by the water). Evergreen tree = *Eternal life;* protection; immortal; always in season; Christmas. Maple tree or maple leaf = *Canada;* sweet; solid; healing; anointed ministry or person. Sugar maple tree = *Promise or opportunity for wealth.*

TREE STUMP—Cut off: Stop; hindered; roots; tenacious; obstacle/unmovable; memory of what once was.

TROPHY—Memorial: Evidence of victory; award; competition; victory in spiritual warfare; prize; striving.

TRUCK—Ministry or Life: Type of truck describes the work. Pickup = *Work.* Tractor-trailer = *Heavy;* powerful. Milk truck = *New believers;* discipleship. Bread truck = *Teaching;* solid foundation.

TRUMPET—Announcement: Preaching; prophesying; warning; call to assemble; worship; the rapture; wake up. Playing taps = *End;* finished; death; sadness; mourning; grief. Type of sound describes the nature of the call or work: Reveille = *Birth;* beginning.

TUNNEL—Transition: Way of escape; troubling experience; trial; hope; faith; darkness to light; transformation.

TURKEY—Foolish: Dumb; clumsy; thanksgiving; pride; struts.

TURTLE—Sure: Steady; sure; guaranteed victory; finish; armour. If native symbol = *Blessing*.

U-TURN— Repentance: Salvation; changed life; change in direction.

UNDERTOW—Undercurrent: Discontent; murmuring; danger of being taken away or taken over; suddenly or unexpected. Hidden danger; behind the scenes; hidden sin.

UNDERWEAR—Covering: Intimate; shame; protection; revealed; uncovered.

UP—Promotion (Spiritual or Natural): Enthusiasm; indication of mood; pride; self-exaltation.

UPSTAIRS—Spiritual: Thought; prayer; spiritual service; promotion.

URINATING—Relief of Pressure: Compelling urge; free; uninhibited; embarrassment if in public view.

VAN—Family: Natural or church family; family ministry; fellowship.

VACUUM CLEANER—Repentance: Cleansing; deliverance ministry; cleaning up the mess; putting in order; preparing a covering.

VEIL—Concealment: Hidden; concealed; covering; deception; without understanding; revealed if curtains are opened or removed.

VEGETABLES—Fruit of One's Labour: Teaching ministry; healthy and balanced spiritual diet; balanced work of service.

VIDEO—Announce: Copy; reproduce; save; store; remember.

VINE—Source: Christ; person; family; city; nation; flesh; entanglement; snare; alive; growing; spreading.

VOLCANO—Eruption: Sudden violent reaction to pressure; emotionally unstable; trouble erupting; God's judgment.

VOLLEYBALL GAME—Worship: Play; sports; team ministry. Back and forth; decision (as in "the ball is in your court").

VULTURE—Scavenger: Unclean; impure; an evil person; awaiting an opportunity to ravish or raid.

WALKING—Progress: Living in the Spirit; living in sin. Making progress; your Christian walk or ministry; walking in the way.

WALL—Barrier: Obstacle; defense; limitation; hindrance; unbelief; protection; restriction; safety; contained. (See FENCE)

WALLET—Safe Place: Power; authority; prosperity.

WARRIOR—See SOLDIER

WASHBASIN—Prayer: Repentance; petition (to God); self-justification (as when Pilate washed his hands at Christ's trial).

WASHBOARD—Rough: Hard correction; cleansing; weariness; hard work; manual labour. Tradition; old-fashioned; old method.

WASHCLOTH—Truth: Doctrine; understanding. Dirty cloth = *False doctrine;* insincere apology; error.

WASP—See HORNET

WATER—Spirit: Word; anointing; refreshing. Muddy or polluted water = *Man's doctrines and ways*; iniquity; haughty spirit; unkind. Troubled water = *Trouble;* worry; sorrow; unclean spirit; healing.

WATER FOUNTAIN—Spirit: Words; spirit of man; Holy Spirit; salvation; source; revival center; place of refreshing.

WATERMELON—Fruit: Refreshing; picnic; reproduction; duplication.

WATER WELL—Source: Heart; spirit of man; the Holy Spirit; refreshing; revival; prayer; hope; wish.

WEASEL—Wicked: Renege on a promise; betrayer; traitor; informant; division; separate.

WEDDING—Covenant: Relationship; agreement; celebrate; unity; becoming one.

WEEDS—Unkempt: Works of the flesh; sin; neglect; laziness; worry; the fullness of iniquity; hindrance; work of the devil; evil thoughts.

WEST—End: Grace; death; last; conformed; sunset of or final stages.

WESTERN—Frontier: Pioneering spirit; spiritual warfare; boldness; challenge; opportunity; wild or rowdy; without boundaries.

WHALE—Special or Large Harvest: Big; large. Belly of the whale = *Hiding from assignment or call in ministry*.

WHEELS—Unending Work: Movement; role; ease; mobile; car; transportation; forward or backward. Wheel within a wheel = *Spirit-driven*; parallel works; unity of the Spirit.

WHITE—Pure: Unblemished; spotless; blameless; righteousness; truth; innocence; plain, without colour. Whitewash = *Cover-up*; hidden.

WHITE OUT—Correction: glory.

WHITEWASH—Cover up; water down.

WIFE—Covenant: Joined; job; business; hobby; Church; dedicated involvement in any activity, such as a job, business, church; help; she may represent herself; helpmate; partner.

WILD GAME—Work: Seeking or doing God's Word and work; sorcery; unbridled or rebellious work.

WIND—Spirit: Holy Spirit; spirit of the word or doctrine; demonic or strong opposition; idle words; storm; freedom; unseen power.

WINDOW—Revealed: Truth; prophecy; revelation; understanding; avenue of blessing; passage of time or light; vulnerable; protection; transparent. If open = *Unprotected* (as in "open door").

WINE (or Strong Drink)—Intoxicant: The blood of the Lord; strong emotion (such as joy, anger, hate, or sorrow); Spirit; spiritual fellowship or communion; truth; witchcraft; delusion; mocker.

WINGS—Spirit: Minister (Prophet); Holy Spirit; shelter; demon; protection; agent or ability to fly or soar. Broken wing = *Hindrance or handicap;* flesh; inability to fly or be free.

WINTER—Barren: Death; dormant; waiting; cold; long, dry spiritual experience; storage.

WITCH—Witchcraft: Control; manipulation; evil influence; evil intent; seduction; nonsubmissive wife; rebellion; slander; gossip; worldly church; evil spirit.

WOLF—Predator: Devourer; Satan; demon of division; sly; group attack; injury or offense; false prophet; evil minister or governor; person seeking his own gain; womanizer. Fangs = *Evil motive*; danger.

WOMAN (ANGEL)—Spirit: Seducing spirit; temptation; deception; witchcraft; God's messenger; angel; one's own self. Name, occupation, function, or appearance can further define.

WOOD—Life or Death: Temporary; flesh; humanity; carnal reasoning; lust; eternal; spiritual building material; ready for sacrifice or use.

WORM—Filth: Corruption; evil; flesh. Life within; Spirit (clean or unclean); sneaky; worthless; bait.

WRESTLING—Striving: Deliverance; resistance; persistence; trial; tribulation; fight; contend for your blessing; controlling spirit attempting to gain control.

YARD—Place of ministry or Life: Outreach ministry. Similar to a room in a house. Front = *Future*. Rear = *Past*. Side = *Current*.

YELLOW—Gift: A gift of God; marriage; family; honour; timidity; fear; cowardly. Welcome home ("a yellow ribbon"); caution.

ZEBRA—Black and White: Similar to a horse; cut-and-dry; half and half; in compromise; camouflage.

ZOO—Strange: Commotion; confusion; chaos; disarray; circus atmosphere; mixture of people or spirits; very busy place; noisy strife; out of nature; preserve; captivity.

RUSS MOYER

Russ Moyer is a missionary in Ontario, Canada. He is the founder and president of Eagle Worldwide Ministries.

Since his arrival in Canada in October of 2000, he has established the Eagle Worldwide Traveling Team, which has ministered in more than sixty churches in North and South America, Europe, and the West Indies, and he has purchased and founded the Eagle Worldwide Retreat and Revival Centre, a beautiful 50+acre parcel of land in Copetown, Ontario. Russ and his wife, Mave, currently pastor Eagles' Nest Fellowship and oversee four other churches that he pioneered in Canada.

Russ was a successful businessman for over twenty-one years and was the recipient of many honours in the business community. He was the founder, president, and CEO of a number of security-related businesses, and at one time employed more than two hundred people. He also was the executive producer and host of a weekly, one-hour television program, which dealt with some of the serious issues facing American families, emphasizing Christian values.

In 1997 he traveled to Pensacola, Florida, to attend the Brownsville Revival School of Ministry. He graduated in December 1999 and was ordained by Ruth Ward Heflin through Calvary Pentecostal Tabernacle in Ashland, Virginia.

Russ is used heavily in the prophetic, deliverance, and healing ministries. He has a heart to see revival in Canada and the nations.

TEACHINGS ON AUDIO

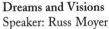

Dreams and Visions
Speaker: Russ Moyer
Teachings Include: In Dreams and Visions; Write the Vision; Dreams and Interpretation
Price: $10.00 CDN $8.00 US
Media Type: CD

Hearing the Voice of the Lord
Speaker: Russ Moyer
Teachings Include: Prayer and Principle; Revelation, Wisdom, and Understanding; Waiting on the Lord
Price: $10.00 CDN $8.00 US
Media Type: CD

Spiritual Gifts
Speaker: Russ Moyer
Teachings Include: Concerning Spiritual Gifts; One Body in Christ; Gifts of the Spirit
Price: $10.00 CDN $8.00 US
Media Type: CD

Eagle Worldwide Resources
P.O. Box 39
Copetown, ON L0R 1J0
Tel. (905) 308-9991   Fax (905) 308-7798
http://www.eagleworldwide.com
enterprises@eagleworldwide.com

TEACHINGS ON AUDIO

The Power of Prayer
Speaker: Russ Moyer
Teachings Include: Intimacy; Prayer and Principle; Types of Prayers; Warriors and Intercessors
Price: $18.00 CDN $16.00 US
Media Type: CD (set of 2)

The Gift of Prophecy
Speaker: Russ Moyer
Teachings Include: The Gift of Prophecy; Eight Channels of Prophecy; Eight Steps to Fulfilling Personal Prophecy
Price: $10.00 CDN $8.00 US
Media Type: CD

Prophetic Delivery
Speaker: Russ Moyer
Teachings Include: Prophetic Lifestyle; Delivery Foundations; How, When, Where, Why, and Why Not
Price: $10.00 CDN $8.00 US
Media Type: CD

Eagle Worldwide Resources
P.O. Box 39
Copetown, ON L0R 1J0
Tel. (905) 308-9991   Fax (905) 308-7798
http://www.eagleworldwide.com
enterprises@eagleworldwide.com

EAGLE WORLDWIDE MINISTRIES

Eagle Worldwide Ministries is a prophetic ministry called to bring revival fire to the nations and to challenge, empower and equip the Church of Jesus Christ with a powerful message of holiness and hope. We focus on the restoration of foundational truths and preparing and equipping the saints for the end time harvest through teaching, impartation and demonstrations of the gifts of the Holy Spirit.

Eagle Worldwide Ministries includes:
- Six churches in Ontario that were birthed through dreams and revelations:
    o The Gathering Place, Aurora, ON
    o Eagle's Nest Fellowship, Copetown, ON
    o Eagle's Nest T.O., Toronto, ON
    o Caleb's Place, Washago, ON
    o Harvest House, St. Catharines, ON
    o The Revival Centre, Hamilton, ON
- The Retreat and Revival Centre, a place where believers can come and be trained, equipped, and prepared for Christian service.
- Eagle Rock Café, our marketplace ministry which reflects the face of the Lord in the community.
- Eagle Worldwide Network of Ministries, which is an apostolic and prophetic network that provides spiritual covering, credentialing, and fellowship to churches, ministries, missionaries, Christian businesspeople and government workers that are pursing their call in church or in the marketplace.

VISIT OUR INTERACTIVE WEBSITE

The Eagle has landed! On the Internet that is. Eagle World-wide is now updated and rocking!! Get the mouse rolling and see what's happening in cyberspace:

http://www.eagleworldwide.com

Bookmark our page and come often for continual updates and new releases. Check out our new Interactive Prophetic section. Find out what the Lord is saying for this week, this month, and through our friends and partners. Do you have a prophetic word you want to share? E-mail it to us right from the Interactive Prophetic page!

Don't forget to click on our calendar for guest speaker information and to see our traveling schedule (the Eagle may land somewhere near you!). Hear audio messages, peruse through our galleries, and even become a member! It's all on the site. Surf the Eagle!

EAGLE WORLDWIDE MINISTRIES
RETREAT AND REVIVAL CENTRE

Summer Camp Meetings
Come and Get in the Glory!

Canada Day through Labour Day Weekend
Every night at 7:00 pm

Every year we hold eight weeks of summer camp at our 50+
acre Retreat Centre. We begin the season with our Parade of
Nations, and hold other events and functions, as well as
performing water baptisms right in our beautiful lakes!
For more information contact us at:
P.O. Box 39
Copetown, ON, L0R 1J0, CANADA
Tel.: (905) 308-9991 Fax: (905) 308-7798
http://www.eagleworldwide.com
enterprises@eagleworldwide.com

Ministry DVDs and CDs available from every service.